How Israelis and Palestinians Negotiate

How Israelis and Palestinians Negotiate

A Cross-Cultural Analysis of the Oslo Peace Process

Edited by Tamara Cofman Wittes

UNITED STATES INSTITUTE OF PEACE PRESS
Washington, D.C.

The views expressed in this book are those of the authors alone. They do not necessarily reflect views of the United States Institute of Peace.

UNITED STATES INSTITUTE OF PEACE
1200 17th Street NW, Suite 200
Washington, DC 20036-3011

First published 2005

Printed in the United States of America

The paper used in this publication meets the minimum requirements of American National Standards for Information Science–Permanence of Paper for Printed Library Materials, ANSI Z39.48-1984.

Library of Congress Cataloging-in-Publication Data

How Israelis and Palestinians negotiate : a cross-cultural analysis of the Oslo
    peace process / edited by Tamara Cofman Wittes.
        p. cm.
    Includes bibliographical references and index.
        ISBN 1-929223-64-1 (cloth : alk. paper) — ISBN 1-929223-63-3 (pbk. :
    alk. paper)
        1. Arab-Israeli conflict—1993—Peace. 2. Negotiation—Cross-cultural
    studies. 3. Israel—Politics and government. 4. Munaòzòzamat al-Taòhràir al-
    Filasòtåinåiyah. 5. National characteristics, Israeli—Political aspects. 6. National
    characteristics, Arab—Political aspects. I. Wittes, Tamara Cofman, 1969–
    II. United States Institute of Peace.

    DS119.7.H688 2005
    956.9405'4—dc22   2004065759

Contents

Foreword

The Israeli-Palestinian conflict has probably generated more published studies than any other ongoing international dispute. In the few years since the Oslo peace process collapsed in violence in September 2000, the postmortems have been legion from participants and observers alike. What can one more analysis of the Oslo years add to our understanding of this intractable conflict?

The answer, in the case of this compact but uncommonly insightful volume, is a surprising amount. This refreshing and revealing collection of essays provides a new lens through which to view the much-discussed failures of Oslo. Culture, according to Tamara Cofman Wittes and her co-authors, did not cause the Oslo breakdown, but it did play an influential, intervening role at several levels: coloring the preferences and strategies of political leaders, shaping the domestic politics that constrained the talks, and molding each side's perceptions of the other's intentions and behavior.

The cultural lens, it turns out, helps us understand much that was mystifying about the outcome of the Oslo peace process. How did an incremental process designed to facilitate gradual confidence building instead produce a downward spiral of mistrust and stalled implementation? This volume provides an explanation rooted in the unfortunate interaction between Israel's national-security-oriented negotiators and the weak, disempowered, and risk-averse Palestinian team. What was the source of the extreme passivity evident in the Palestinian negotiating style, which American mediators found so maddening and which led President Clinton to later blame Palestinian leader Yasser Arafat for the breakdown of talks at Camp David in July 2000? Omar Dajani, in his groundbreaking contribution to this volume, explains the cultural, historical, and political roots of the PLO's dysfunctional negotiating behavior. But, as Aharon Klieman makes clear, the fault did not lie entirely on one side of the negotiating table. In a critique that is as sophisticated as it is iconoclastic, Klieman delineates two subcultures among Israeli negotiators, a diplomatic- and a security-oriented subculture. He argues that Ehud Barak's attempt to embrace both approaches simultaneously fueled Palestinian suspicions and proved profoundly inept.

Framing the contributions from Dajani and Klieman are an introductory chapter by Wittes that details the purposes, and limitations, of a cultural analysis of negotiations; a succinct overview by William Quandt of the Oslo years and the multiple factors in the domestic, regional, and international environments that shaped the talks, not least the role of American mediation; and a conclusion in which Wittes brings together the stories of the two sides, revealing how Israeli and Palestinian negotiating styles interacted in ways that were particularly, and tragically, counterproductive. She then draws lessons for future negotiators and mediators, focusing on how leaders must work together to overcome the deleterious effects that cultural baggage can bring to peace negotiations. In discussing the role of ethnic identity in the Oslo negotiations and highlighting some parallels between the Israeli-Palestinian conflict and other identity conflicts, Wittes broadens the relevance of this study beyond Middle East specialists to encompass the broader community of scholars and practitioners in the field of negotiation, particularly those dealing with entrenched ethnic conflicts.

This book is the seventh in a series of volumes published by the United States Institute of Peace about the negotiating styles of different countries. Previous volumes in the series have explored Chinese, Russian, North Korean, Japanese, French, and German negotiating behavior. These books reflect the Institute's conviction that negotiating approaches to international conflict resolution, as well as less adversarial diplomatic or business encounters, will achieve greater success when negotiators from different nations and cultures better "read" the intentions of their counterparts over a green baize table. In the case of the Israeli-Palestinian conflict, this volume's contributors note, the primary difficulty in intercultural understanding is not cultural ignorance but the ironies of cultural interactions—the ways in which each side's prior history, and their shared history of conflict, shapes their interactions across the negotiating table.

This volume represents a slight departure from the Institute's cross-cultural negotiation series in that it is the first to examine in detail the negotiating behavior on both sides of an international conflict. This dyadic approach provides a richer portrait of the Oslo process than would be provided by a focus on a single side, and also shows how national negotiating styles can play out differently with different interlocutors.

The volume also integrates cultural analysis into the broader canvas of the negotiating environment by treating culture as an intervening variable, one that filters the varying effects of bureaucratic jockeying, international mediation, domestic party politics, and the influence of public opinion. Placing culture in this intermediary role advances the theoretical understanding of culture's role in conflict resolution, a core goal of the Institute's cross-cultural negotiation project. In so doing, the present volume not only adds breadth to our canvas of national negotiating styles but also builds on two previous conceptual works published by the Institute: Raymond Cohen's *Negotiating across Cultures* and Kevin Avruch's *Culture and Conflict Resolution*.

Culture, of course, is not the primary determinant of a country's negotiating behavior, and in many cases its influence may be marginal relative to other factors. The Institute's intent has been to draw attention to, but not to exaggerate, culture's role in shaping international negotiations. But, as this volume's innovative approach reveals, culture's influence is pervasive, and may be evident less in independent effects than in the coloring of other principal dimensions of negotiating behavior. Because of this interweaving of culture's impact into all aspects of the negotiating environment, negotiators often ascribe to ill will or incompatible preferences decisions that may instead by explained by cultural miscues.

In its inventive analysis of the ill-fated Oslo peace process, this volume will help negotiators, mediators, and analysts better understand the process's failings, and thereby will help to improve the chances of success in the next round of Israeli-Palestinian negotiations.

Richard H. Solomon, President
United States Institute of Peace

Acknowledgments

I am lucky to have attracted to this project three stellar contributors, William Quandt, Omar Dajani, and Aharon Klieman. For each of them in different ways, this project represented a departure from their usual modes of thinking about the Israeli-Palestinian conflict. I am grateful for their willingness to stretch in new directions, and for allowing me to benefit from and build upon their endeavors.

This book is only one small manifestation of the immeasurable contribution made by the United States Institute of Peace to the understanding and amelioration of international conflict. I am deeply grateful for the sponsorship and support of the Institute and its president, Richard H. Solomon, whose leadership has enabled continuous and considerable growth in research into culture and conflict resolution. To the Institute's director of Research and Studies, Paul Stares, I owe thanks for giving me the freedom to pursue this project during my tenure at the Institute, and for invaluable professional mentoring throughout. My successor at the Institute, Scott Lasensky, cheerfully picked up the project and shepherded it to completion. Elise Murphy handled administration and logistics with aplomb. The Institute's able Publications Department greased all wheels to get the book to press in record time. The incomparable Nigel Quinney, virtual custodian of the Institute's book series on cross-cultural negotiations, was my sounding board, guide, and adjutant at every stage. The book's arguments were greatly improved by the constructive comments of Raymond Cohen, Samuel Lewis, Shibley Telhami, Marc Ross, Ed Abington, David Makovsky, Rob Malley, Philip Mattar, and Michael Barnett, as well as the anonymous reviewers for the United States Institute of Peace Press. Martin Indyk and Ken Pollack at the Saban Center for Middle East Policy at the Brookings Institution allowed me the necessary time to complete the volume. As always, my husband Ben's grace, generosity, and genuine interest sustained my efforts throughout.

Contributors

Tamara Cofman Wittes is a research fellow at the Saban Center for Middle East Policy at the Brookings Institution. She was previously a Middle East specialist at the United States Institute of Peace, where she conducted and supervised research on the Arab-Israeli peace process, regional security, and U.S. relations with the Muslim world. She was one of the first recipients of the Rabin-Peres Peace Award, established by President Bill Clinton in 1997. Her work has been published in numerous journals, including *Policy Review, Political Science Quarterly,* the *Weekly Standard,* and the *Chronicle of Higher Education.*

❖ ❖ ❖

Omar M. Dajani is assistant professor of law at the University of the Pacific, McGeorge School of Law. Previously, he served as legal adviser to the Palestinian negotiating team in peace talks with Israel from 1999 to 2001, and then as political adviser to United Nations Special Coordinator Terje Roed-Larsen. He received his BA from Northwestern University and his JD from Yale Law School.

Aharon Klieman is professor of international relations in the Department of Political Science at Tel Aviv University, where he holds the Dr. Nahum Goldmann Chair in Diplomacy and is director of the Abba Eban Graduate Program in Diplomatic Studies. He has held visiting appointments at Georgetown University, the University of Chicago, the University of Denver, and the University of Michigan. He has also participated in track-two diplomacy within the Middle East peace process. His books include *Israel and the World after Forty Years* (1990), *Constructive Ambiguity in Middle East Peace-Making* (1999), and *Compromising Palestine: A Guide to Final Status Negotiations* (2000).

William B. Quandt is Edward R. Stettinius Professor of Politics at the University of Virginia, where he previously served as vice provost for international affairs. In the course of a distinguished career, he has served on the staff of the National Security Council, participated in the negotiations that led to the Camp David Treaty, taught at the University of Pennsylvania, UCLA, and MIT, worked for the RAND Corporation, and held the position of senior fellow at the Brookings Institution. He has written extensively on the Middle East and U.S. policy toward the Arab-Israeli conflict.

How Israelis and Palestinians Negotiate

1

Introduction

◆◆◆◆◆◆◆◆◆◆◆◆◆◆◆◆◆

The Goal of

◆◆◆◆◆◆◆◆◆◆◆◆

Cultural Analysis

◆◆◆◆◆◆◆◆◆◆◆◆◆◆◆◆◆

Tamara Cofman Wittes

The United States Institute of Peace's project on cross-cultural negotiations is a long-standing investment by the Institute in improving the capacity of the United States and other countries for peaceful settlement of disputes. It confronts one of the enduring challenges of international conflict resolution: no matter what interests the two sides in a negotiation might share, no matter how high the stakes for successful agreement, talks can fail—or produce agreements that fail—simply because cultural differences preclude clear communication and shared understanding between the negotiators. The Institute's interest in this issue began with Senior Fellow Raymond Cohen, whose 1988 tenure at the Institute resulted in *Negotiating across Cultures,* a second edition of which was published in 1997 and has become a defining work in the field of intercultural negotiation. The Institute's commitment to the topic was strengthened by Richard Solomon, who became its president in 1993. As a scholar at the RAND Corporation, Solomon prepared the classified study that later became *Chinese Negotiating Behavior: Pursuing Interests through "Old Friends."* The book was originally issued by RAND in 1995 and was republished by the Institute in an expanded edition in 1999. The Institute has now published a total of seven books in a series on cross-cultural negotiation, including studies on the negotiating behavior of Japan, North Korea, Russia, Germany, and France, as well as Kevin Avruch's theoretical study, *Culture and Conflict Resolution.*[1]

In exploring how cultural differences affect international interactions, this Institute series has repeatedly struggled with definitions of culture, one of the most widely contested concepts in the social science literature. Raymond Cohen sees culture as "human software," as "a grammar for organizing reality, for imparting meaning to the world." As such, he noted, culture "is made up of ideas, meanings, conventions, and assumptions."[2] Cohen ascribes to culture three key features: it is a quality of society, not of individuals; it is acquired through socialization; and it subsumes "every area of social life."[3]

But Kevin Avruch notes that culture can take on either of two meanings, alternatives that have entirely opposite implications for the study of culture in negotiations. "Generic culture," Avruch writes, "directs our attention to universal attributes of human behavior—to 'human nature.' Local culture directs our attention to diversity, difference, and particularism." Ignoring differences in local culture, Avruch points out, means that "negotiation looks the same everywhere. But sometimes you just have to speak louder and slower." This simplified concept of international negotiation is precisely what the study of cross-cultural negotiations is meant to combat by improving theories of negotiation through the introduction of local cultural differences as a relevant variable.

Using a concept of "local culture," however, carries its own dangers, Avruch cautions: "[T]o ignore generic culture is . . . to lose sight of the possibility of intertranslatability across local cultures," to give up on the possibility of reaching intercultural understandings through negotiations.[4] From Avruch, then, we can see that understanding the proper place of local culture in the negotiations process requires modesty, but also a keen eye for differences in meaning that negotiators themselves might well miss in their drive to reach what they believe is common agreement.

But even defining what Avruch would call local culture, cultures specific to different social groups (or, for our subject matter, nations), is a tricky and much-debated business. For the purposes of this volume, we shall set out culture as *the product of the experiences of individuals within a given social group, including its representations in images, narratives, myths, and patterns of behavior (traditions), and the meanings of those representations as transmitted among the group's members over time and through experience.* This definition allows, importantly, for individuals within a group to be differently situated by class, race, or other social attributes, such that identifiable subcultures can exist within a broader recognized culture.[5]

In analyzing the influence of culture and cultural differences on peace negotiations, we are concerned more particularly with *political culture,* which Gabriel Almond and Sydney Verba famously define as "attitudes toward the political system and its various parts, and attitudes toward the role of the self in the system."[6] But given that the groups we are concerned with (Israelis and Palestinians) are ethnonational groups, their political cultures are heavily shaped by their ethnonational identities. For that reason, the narratives of each group's origins, of its relations with its historical rival and other national groups, and of its modern political dilemmas are of particular interest and attention for us in the analysis that follows.

In emphasizing the ethnonational content of Israeli and Palestinian political cultures, we do not mean to exclude other elements that make up their cultures, nor do we mean to reduce the political cultures of these two groups to the meanings of their iconic symbols (say, Masada for Israelis or Deir Yassin for Palestinians).[7] But the study of ethnic conflicts shows that the symbolic ingredients of ethnic identity, and particularly the status over time of issues, individuals, or places that symbolize something important about an ethnic group's national narrative, heavily color such communities' political culture. Indeed, ethnic identity and its symbolic manifestations have been shown to affect groups' perceptions of issues central to their conflict, such as the prerequisites of security, the intentions of their adversary, and the definition and purposes of political power and sovereignty.[8] Thus, in an identity conflict such as the Palestinian-Israeli one, the cultural variables that complicate the negotiating process affect not only the communications between the negotiators but many other aspects of the negotiations process as well, suffusing, ultimately, even the substantive issues—land, money, political power—that are themselves under discussion.

Culture in the Oslo Peace Process

Because culture so colors the mutual perceptions and interactions of ethnic groups in conflict, it would be simplistic in the extreme to argue that cross-cultural miscommunications are the main story of culture's importance to the attempt at Israeli-Palestinian rapprochement assessed in this volume.

Furthermore, none of this volume's authors believes that cultural differences between Israelis and Palestinians are the primary cause for the parties' failure to agree on a negotiated solution to their century-old conflict.

The failure of the Oslo process, which ran from 1993 through 2000, has already been dissected in several studies by analysts and by participants in the negotiations.[9] In particular, the failure of the Camp David final-status talks in July 2000 has been the subject of voluminous journalistic and partisan disputation.[10] The existing literature yields a laundry list of potentially blameworthy factors: botched American mediation, inattention to confidence-building measures, a failure to attract Arab and international support, the gradualist structure for the peace process created by the 1993 Oslo agreement, and the personalities of, inter alia, Yasser Arafat, Binyamin Netanyahu, Ehud Barak, and Bill Clinton. With so many errors and deficiencies to choose from, it is perhaps less remarkable that the Oslo peace process ultimately failed, and more remarkable that any of the negotiations during this period succeeded.

One also need not argue that attention to the influence of culture in interethnic negotiations means assuming that cultural differences themselves present gargantuan barriers to agreement. As William Quandt points out in chapter 2, all international negotiations involve overcoming differences in communication to achieve common agreement. A determinist view of culture's influence on the negotiating process would suggest that most, if not all, international negotiations should fail, an empirically unsustainable claim. Avruch's reminder of the existence of a generic human culture also serves as a corrective to such an analytic error.

Moreover, it is not mutual cultural ignorance that we claim has complicated the Israeli-Palestinian negotiations. All three of my coauthors emphasize, in fact, that Israelis and Palestinians are not cultural strangers but share an intimate acquaintance and mutual history that is nonetheless a source of great controversy and mutual grievance. Over the course of their century of conflict, those Israelis and Palestinians who have engaged in negotiations have evolved sophisticated appreciations of each other's national narrative. The Oslo process began with mutual recognition by Israel and the Palestine Liberation Organization (PLO) of each other's fundamental relevance and legitimacy as the political embodiment of Jewish and Palestinian national claims, respectively. But this sensitivity has proved insufficient to enable the sides to reach a negotiated agreement. Our research suggests that one factor contributing to this insufficiency is that each community's collective pathologies, developed over the course of the conflict, continue to shape and in many ways constrain the negotiators' well-developed style of interaction.

Rather than presenting culture as a definitive explanatory variable, the authors of this volume are arguing for the relevance of culture to the broader story of the Israeli-Palestinian negotiations, beyond the narrow question of face-to-face encounters between negotiators, and for the idea that insights into the intercultural dynamics of the negotiations will provide valuable lessons for future Israeli and Palestinian negotiators and, more broadly, for scholars of negotiation and ethnic conflict.

As the authors in this volume reveal through their detailed analysis of Israeli and Palestinian negotiating styles, culture plays a subtler and more multifaceted role than merely provoking misunderstanding. Cultural factors influenced the assessments and decisions of individual leaders and negotiators, shaped the domestic institutions and political environment in which policy decisions on negotiation were made and carried out, and shaped each party's perception of their relative balance of power and how best to respond to it. Culture's role in this case, and in other negotiations of identity conflicts, is best understood as an intervening variable that operates at different levels, through the impact of cultural identity and cultural categories of thinking on political leaders, on the domestic politics of each side that constrain the negotiations, and on each side's evaluation of the other's beliefs and intentions regarding the conflict being negotiated. This intermediary and multidimensional role for culture will be explored in greater detail in the book's conclusion.

It is in part because of the complications introduced in considering a case of ethnonational conflict, in which cultural identity is at the heart of the dispute under negotiation, that this volume represents a departure from the Institute's previous work on this topic. Previous studies in this series have examined a single country's approach to a variety of negotiations with different partners on different topics. In this volume, we approach the question of national differences in negotiations through the prism of a *dyadic interaction*—the Oslo peace talks between Israel and the PLO. By focusing on a single country's negotiating behavior without reference to its interlocutor, previous studies sometimes ended by reducing the valuation of cultural variables to either-or dichotomies, such as the distinction between high-context societies (wherein the identity and social position of a negotiator may be more important to interpreting his meaning than the content of his communication) and low-context societies (wherein the content of communication typically trumps its social context).[11] Considering a single nation's cultural behavior in isolation risks essentializing the scholarly view of the society under discussion, and at the extreme can send the analyst in the direction of the "national character" or "modal personality" studies popular several decades ago.[12] Examining a dyadic interaction, in contrast, allows the analyst to examine cultural variables in a relative fashion, preventing reductionism and helping create a spectrum of values for cultural variables to replace the dichotomies still prevalent in the literature.[13] Moreover, examining an interaction between two sides in great detail facilitates thicker description of the cultural context for the negotiations: the way in which cultural factors shape each side's approach to negotiations generally, to their historical relationship with their interlocutors, and to the specific issues under dispute. Finally, studying a single case of negotiation between two national parties reveals how the two national styles interact—a particularly relevant angle when studying negotiations between ethnic groups in conflict, whose national identities and cultural ingredients are interrelated and often defined to a great degree by reference to one another. The dyadic approach reveals, for example, that Israel's habitually forceful, divide-and-rule approach to negotiating might be generally effective with Arab states and outside powers, but spectacularly ineffective when interacting with the Palestinians' culturally, historically, and institutionally determined approach to negotiating with Israel.

This volume roots its discussion of culture's role in a detailed examination of Israeli and Palestinian negotiating behavior from the outset of the secret Oslo talks that led to the Declaration of Principles (signed in Washington, DC, on September 13, 1993), through the Camp David summit in July 2000 and the abortive Taba negotiations that continued almost until the end of Bill Clinton's presidency in early 2001. In chapter 2, William Quandt surveys this history of rapprochement between Israel and the PLO and discusses the international and domestic political factors, most notably U.S. mediation, that facilitated the talks and influenced their progress and ultimate outcome.

In chapter 3, Omar Dajani, a former legal adviser to the Palestinian negotiating team and a former UN mediator, undertakes a study of Palestinian negotiating behavior, which by itself has frequently baffled Israeli interlocutors and outside mediators and contributed to Israeli suspicion of Palestinian intentions with respect to peace. Dajani reveals how elements of Palestinian identity and national development have shaped the structure of the Palestinian national movement's leadership, its conduct of the negotiations, and its attitude toward core subjects at issue in the talks, producing an indecisive and dysfunctional policy process within the PLO that crippled its ability to negotiate effectively.

In chapter 4, Aharon Klieman, a distinguished analyst of Israel's international relations, traces the impact on the Israeli-Palestinian negotiations of a long-standing cultural clash within the Israeli political elite: a struggle between diplomatic and security subcultures for dominance over Israel's negotiating style and strategy. By limning this battle as it played out within and among Israel's political leadership and as it affected Israeli domestic politics, Klieman reveals how Israelis' communal identity and self-perception relative to their Arab neighbors has deeply and decisively affected the Israeli approach to negotiations with the Palestinians in ways that can only be described as shortsighted and ultimately, in the final status negotiations, counterproductive.

In chapter 5, I draw on the findings of the previous chapters to illustrate culture's influence, as an intervening variable, on the international, domestic, and individual levels of analysis in interethnic negotiations. I show how, in particular, negotiations in identity conflicts such as the Israeli-Palestinian case display an extreme sensitivity to domestic pressures that complicates the two-level game of the negotiating process and raises the bar for success. The chapter also provides some lessons for future negotiators in the Israeli-Palestinian dispute and in other ethnic conflicts.

Rather than arguing, as a facile prescription, that intercultural understanding is the missing key that can unlock the door to Israeli-Palestinian peace, this volume suggests that a better understanding by political leaders and negotiators of how culture shapes their operating environment might improve their odds of success the next time Israelis and Palestinians are able to face each other across the negotiating table.

Notes

1. Richard H. Solomon, *Chinese Negotiating Behavior: Pursuing Interests through "Old Friends"* (Washington, DC: United States Institute of Peace Press, 1999); Michael Blaker, Paul Giarra, and Ezra Vogel, *Case Studies in Japanese*

Negotiating Behavior (Washington, DC: United States Institute of Peace Press, 2002); Scott Snyder, *Negotiating on the Edge: North Korean Negotiating Behavior* (Washington, DC: United States Institute of Peace Press, 1999); Jerrold L. Schecter, *Russian Negotiating Behavior: Continuity and Transition* (Washington, DC: United States Institute of Peace Press, 1998); W. R. Smyser, *How Germans Negotiate: Logical Goals, Practical Solutions* (Washington, DC: United States Institute of Peace Press, 2003); and Charles Cogan, *French Negotiating Behavior: Dealing with La Grande Nation* (Washington, DC: United States Institute of Peace Press, 2003). The Institute has also turned the spotlight on U.S. diplomats; see *U.S. Negotiating Behavior,* United States Institute of Peace Special Report 94 (Washington, DC: United States Institute of Peace, October 2002).

2. Raymond Cohen, *Negotiating across Cultures: International Communication in an Interdependent World,* rev. ed. (Washington, DC: United States Institute of Peace Press, 1997), 12.

3. Cohen, *Negotiating across Cultures*, 10.

4. Kevin Avruch, *Culture and Conflict Resolution* (Washington, DC: United States Institute of Peace Press, 1998), 10.

5. This definition draws heavily on Theodore Schwartz's definition as cited and amended by Avruch in *Culture and Conflict Resolution*, 17–19.

6. Gabriel A. Almond and Sidney Verba, *The Civic Culture: Political Attitudes and Democracy in Five Nations* (Princeton, NJ: Princeton University Press, 1963), 13.

7. Masada is the site of a Herodian palace, but more famously of a mass suicide by early-first-century Jewish guerrillas who preferred death to capture by the Romans. Masada is thus a symbol for modern Israelis of resilience and determination in the face of continual besiegement. Deir Yassin was a Palestinian village, about one hundred of whose inhabitants were massacred by Jewish fighters during the 1948 war that established the state of Israel. It is a concrete symbol for Palestinians of the 1948 *nakba* (catastrophe) and of how Zionism's realization was their own victimization.

8. See Tamara Cofman Wittes, "Symbols and Security in Ethnic Conflict: Confidence-Building in the Palestinian-Israeli Peace Process, 1993–1995" (PhD dissertation, Georgetown University, 2000), 39–51; Loring M. Danforth, *The Macedonian Conflict: Ethnic Nationalism in a Transnational World* (Princeton, NJ: Princeton University Press, 1995); Mary Kay Gilliland, "Nationalism and Ethnogenesis in the Former Yugoslavia," in *Ethnic Identity: Creation, Conflict, and Accommodation,* ed. Lola Romanucci-Ross and George A. De Vos (Walnut Creek, CA: Sage Publications, 1995) at 203–204; and Stuart Kaufman, "Spiraling to Ethnic War: Elites, Masses, and Moscow in Moldova's Civil War," in *Nationalism and Ethnic Conflict,* ed. Michael E. Brown, et al. (Cambridge, MA: MIT Press, 1997), 169–199.

9. Third-party accounts (post–Camp David) include Charles Enderlin, *Shattered Dreams: The Failure of the Peace Process in the Middle East, 1995–2002,* trans. Susan Fairfield (New York: Other Press, 2003); Robert Rothstein, Moshe Maoz, and Khalil Shikaki, eds., *The Israeli-Palestinian Peace Process: Oslo and the Lessons of Failure—Perspectives, Predicaments, and Prospects* (East Sussex, UK: Sussex Academic Press, 2002); and William Quandt, *Peace Process: American Diplomacy and the Arab-Israeli Conflict since 1967,* rev. ed. (Berkeley: University of California Press, 2001).

First-person accounts include Martin Indyk, *Unintended Consequences: The Clinton Years in the Middle East* (New York: Frank Knopf, forthcoming spring 2005); Dennis Ross, *The Missing Peace: The Inside Story of the Fight for Middle East Peace* (New York: Farrar, Straus, Giroux, 2004); Eytan Bentsur, *Making Peace: A First-Hand Account of the Arab-Israeli Peace Process* (Westport, CT: Praeger, 2001); Yossi Beilin, *Touching Peace: From the Oslo Accord to a Final Agreement,* trans. Philip Simpson (London: Weidenfeld & Nicholson, 1999); Uri Savir, *The Process: 1,100 Days That Changed the Middle East* (New York: Random House, 1998); Mahmoud Abbas, *Through Secret Channels: The Road to Oslo—Senior PLO Leader Abu Mazen's Revealing Story of the Negotiations with Israel* (Reading, UK: Garnet Publishing, 1997); Shimon Peres, *Battling for Peace: A Memoir* (New York: Random House, 1995).

10. See, most notably, Robert Malley and Hussein Agha, "Camp David: A Tragedy of Errors," *New York Review of Books* 48, no. 13, August 9, 2001, 59; Benny Morris, "Camp David and After: An Exchange. 1. An Interview with Ehud Barak," *New York Review of Books* 49, no. 10, June 13, 2002, 42, and replies and rejoinders June 13, 2002, and June 27, 2002.

11. See Edward T. Hall and Mildred Reed Hall, *Hidden Differences: Doing Business with the Japanese* (Garden City, NY: Anchor Press/Doubleday, 1987).

12. The concept of discerning national character according to shared cultural practices was developed inter alia by Ralph Linton in *The Cultural Background of Personality* (New York: Appleton-Century-Crofts, 1945) and explicated in his foreword to Abram Kardiner and others, *The Psychological Frontiers of Society* (New York: Columbia University Press, 1945), vii–viii. A example of such studies in the Middle Eastern context is Raphael Patai, *The Arab Mind* (New York: Scribner, 1973).

13. Indeed, this dyadic approach follows in the tradition of Raymond Cohen's pioneering work in the field of cross-cultural negotiations, *Culture and Conflict in Egyptian-Israeli Relations: A Dialogue of the Deaf* (Bloomington: Indiana University Press, 1990). Cohen's analysis of Arab-Israeli negotiations, however, focuses on the linguistic and other differences in meaning evident in face-to-face encounters by diplomats.

2

Israeli-Palestinian

❖❖❖❖❖❖❖❖❖❖❖❖❖❖❖❖❖❖❖❖❖❖❖❖❖

Peace Talks

❖❖❖❖❖❖❖❖❖❖❖❖❖❖❖❖❖

From Oslo

❖❖❖❖❖❖❖❖❖❖❖❖

to Camp David II

❖❖❖❖❖❖❖❖❖❖❖❖❖❖❖❖❖❖❖

William B. Quandt

During the 1990s, the peace process between Israel and the Palestinians was something like a roller coaster. Moments of despair and violence alternated with moments of hope and creativity. Issues that had long been avoided were tackled with an unprecedented degree of seriousness. At the same time, however, old suspicions lingered, distrust was never far from the surface, and radicals in both camps were prepared to do all they could to undermine the hard work of the more moderate leaders who had decided to gamble on peace.

By the early part of 2001, this decade-long effort came to a sudden halt amid mutual accusations and recriminations and a seemingly unstoppable cycle of violence. The precise story of why this search for a negotiated settlement failed cannot yet be fully told, since many of the crucial details are still missing, but the overall picture is reasonably clear. The purpose of this chapter is to provide a basis for understanding the negotiating process that took place during the period from early 1993 through January 2001. Along the way, some needed background will be provided, and the story will be brought up-to-date through 2003.

The focus will be on the negotiations between Israelis and Palestinians, but it must always be understood that these talks did not take place in a vacuum. The United States, for example, was an important player in this process, sometimes pushing the parties forward, offering incentives and reassurances, and sometimes holding back for fear that its own actions might discourage the local parties from making the hard decisions that confronted them. In addition, Israel throughout this period was also considering negotiations with Syria and was trying to figure out what to do with its military presence in Lebanon. Finally, this episode of negotiations took place in the aftermath of the Gulf War of 1990–91, a rise of Islamic radicalism in many parts of the Middle East, and the end of the Cold War.

Historical Legacies and Cultural Predispositions

When parties have been locked in conflict for long periods, it is often tempting to conclude that they are trapped by the weight of history or by clashing cultural imperatives. Observers sometimes argue that conflicts of this sort cannot be resolved by conventional diplomatic efforts. And yet conflict resolution, when successful, always involves overcoming some historical legacies and bridging certain cultural divides. It is not at all obvious that these divisive factors carry more weight in the Israeli-Palestinian conflict than they did, for example, in the Franco-German rivalry of an earlier era. Still, we need to at least sketch the outlines of how history and culture affect the context in which negotiations take place.

On a very general level, it is possible to identify some broad themes in Israeli and Palestinian history and culture that affect the conduct of diplomacy. On the Israeli side, there is a deep feeling that the entire enterprise of modern Zionism, the creation of a Jewish state in the Holy Land, is legitimate—whether for religious reasons or because of the unique trauma of the Holocaust that befell Jewish populations in Europe with the rise of Nazism. Jews not only have the right to a state, most Israelis will argue, but also had no alternative to the path they took to create and defend it. Since Arabs and Palestinians were initially unwilling to recognize Israel's existence, Israel was under no obligation to make concessions on issues such as refugees or borders. War, they maintain, was forced on Israel. The Arabs, by refusing Israel a place in its historic homeland, were the aggressors, not the Zionists.

On the Palestinian side, the dominant view has been that Israel is an illegitimate outcome of the Western colonial era and that Palestinians should not have to bear the burden of compensating Jews for Hitler's crimes. Palestinians typically see themselves as victims of a historical process in which power trumped claims of justice. The *nakba,* or "catastrophe," of 1948–49, which resulted in some seven to eight hundred thousand Palestinians losing their homes, has left a bitter legacy among Palestinians. Not only is Israel held responsible for this traumatic loss, but also Israel has refused for decades to accept that Palestinian refugees have the right to choose between returning to their homes and being compensated for their losses. In addition, Israeli land expropriation and the establishment of Jewish settlements throughout the territories held by Israel since 1967 have touched a deep historical sensitivity and fear. There is also bitterness at the lack of effective Arab and Muslim support for the Palestinian cause.

With this background in mind, it might seem that Israelis and Palestinians would never seek to resolve their conflict through negotiations. But over the years, each side has had to accept that the other party will not go away, nor will it abandon its claims to a political identity in Palestine/ Eretz Yisrael. And at least for a few pragmatists, this recognition of competing stubborn claims to the land led to a realization that history and arguments about rights and wrongs could never resolve the conflict. In fact, during the early negotiations of the Oslo Accords, the negotiators decided not to debate historical issues, realizing that neither could convert the other to its views of the past.

Even with history relegated to the sidelines, there are ways in which the past and cultural legacies intrude on negotiations. Israelis are inevitably sensitive to anything that questions the right of Israel to exist as a predominantly Jewish state. Thus, the issue of a return of Palestinian refugees triggers an almost irrational fear; the issue of borders and security also touches on the matter of the state's viability. In light of the history of Zionist colonization of the land, the matter of settlements is also of great sensitivity. And, of course, Jerusalem has a place of special religious meaning for all Jewish Israelis.

The suicide bombings that extremist Palestinians launched with such devastating effect in 2001 also convinced many Israelis that Palestinian intentions were not limited to the end of the occupation but rather were aimed at the murder of Jews and the extermination of the Jewish state.

Israelis who had been tempted to support a negotiated solution to the conflict were so horrified by the spate of terrorist attacks against civilians that they became outspoken opponents of negotiations.

On the Palestinian side, a major hurdle to overcome has been accepting what was previously unacceptable—the idea of sharing historical Palestine and tempering their own claims of justice with a recognition of Jewish claims. This shift did not come easily or quickly for Palestinians, but during the 1970s and 1980s the formal position of the Palestine Liberation Organization (PLO) began to change. In 1988, for the first time the PLO recognized Israel's right to exist within the 1967 lines. From the Palestinian standpoint, this amounted to ceding the claim to nearly 80 percent of British-mandated Palestine. The idea of giving up even more was anathema. In addition, Palestinians found it difficult to address the "right of return" in anything less than the most adamant manner. While in private many were prepared to say that few refugees would actually choose to return to Israel proper, the right of refugees to do so was seen as nearly inviolate. Almost no Palestinian politician was prepared to discuss in public the realistic options that might confront Palestinian refugees as part of a negotiated settlement, and this indeed turned out to be one of the issues on which the negotiations of 2000 foundered.

These historically rooted sensitivities on both sides had a clear effect on negotiations. Neither side was ready to explore possible compromises in public for fear of the backlash from its own constituents, who had been nurtured on a self-righteous view of the issues at stake. So negotiations required secrecy and discipline; both sides were fearful of leaks that would make them look weak. An "Alphonse-Gaston" quality pervaded the talks: "If you want me to make concessions, you must prepare the way by making yours first. Only then can I afford to take the risks of tipping my hand." The underlying assumption of confidence-building measures—that each party would and could take small, unilateral steps toward the other to show its good intentions—was simply not part of the actual negotiating repertoire of either side.

The power disparity between Israel and the Palestinians also affected the negotiations. On the local level, Israel was overwhelmingly in the commanding position. This made it difficult for the Palestinians to extract concessions. Palestinians were always worried that any move they made in Israel's direction might be seen as a sign of weakness. So Palestinians clung to their strong suit—international legitimacy, UN resolutions, and broad principles of international law. Perhaps they felt that, by evoking these themes, they would eventually rally the international community to their side to offset Israel's power advantage.

In contrast, Israelis felt very powerful vis-à-vis the Palestinians but were worried about the broader Arab and international setting, where Israel had few allies. Any sign of flexibility toward the Palestinians might lead to accelerating demands for more and more concessions from countries that were seen as congenitally hostile to Israel and Zionism. Thus, a negotiator such as Israeli prime minister Ehud Barak was reluctant to preview any of the concessions he was prepared to consider—even President Clinton was kept in the dark—hoping that he could put together an entire package in secret and then present it to his own skeptical public and the rest of the world as a done deal. To the Palestinians, this negotiating ploy, anchored in domestic political anxieties as well as a concern with international public opinion, seemed more like a diktat than a negotiation.

As the stronger party, Israel also had a tendency to act as if a display of military power might bring the Palestinians to their senses. Even a moderate such as Shimon Peres felt the need to show toughness in the spring of 1996, when facing both an upsurge in Palestinian terror attacks and a challenge from a hawkish political opponent, Benjamin Netanyahu. The result of Peres's attacks in Lebanon, however, was counterproductive. He lost the election and alienated moderate Palestinians at the same time. Later in the 1990s, the use of targeted assassinations against militant Palestinians by Israel often served to set back the negotiating process rather than forcing the Palestinians to come to terms. It was as if the Israelis felt the need to assert their military superiority, and the Palestinians felt the need to show that they could not be easily intimidated by such displays of power.

Israelis and Palestinians also differ over how international law relates to peacemaking. For Israelis, especially in the period when Menachem Begin was prime minister, there often has been a remarkably tenacious preoccupation with words and texts, even when the negotiators profess to distrust entirely the intentions of the other side. As a result, negotiation often involves mind-bending discussions of the meanings of words and what might happen in various hypothetical contingencies. Some of the negotiated agreements, such as the Oslo II Accord of 1995, are extremely lengthy, as if by covering every conceivable base, closing every loophole, the agreement might be made to work.

On the Palestinian side, there is much more emphasis on key principles —the "right of self-determination," the "right of return," the "inadmissibility of the acquisition of territory by war"—as if the statement of these principles will shift the scales of justice in their direction. Palestinians find the pedantic style of legalism engaged in by some Israeli negotiators frustrating to deal with, since it can come across as a way of avoiding the key issues in dispute. Still, with these significant differences at play, the two sides have nonetheless managed to negotiate a significant number of agreements, and in doing so have learned something about the sensitivities on both sides.

Diplomacy, of course, is specifically designed as a means for working through these issues of historical baggage, fears, distrust, and cultural differences. Diplomats are trained to try to see things from diverse perspectives, to craft positions that allow each side to save face, and to use international norms and law in creative ways to solve problems. Nothing in the Israeli-Palestinian conflict should have made it impossible to work toward agreements. But in the 1990s, Israeli-Palestinian diplomacy ultimately failed. The reasons, however, go beyond history and culture. At most, it is fair to say that politicians felt constrained by history and culture primarily in their public stance with their own constituents. The inability to publicly question certain established positions—Jerusalem for Israelis and refugee rights for Palestinians, for example—meant that neither public was well prepared when the moment for compromise came in late 2000. But there were other reasons for the failure of these negotiations as well, and we will briefly note some of them.

Additional Reasons for the Failure of Diplomacy

First, and perhaps most obvious, is the intrinsic difficulty of finding mutually acceptable solutions to such issues as Jerusalem, refugee claims, security, and borders. This is not to say that these issues cannot be resolved, but simply that the difficulty of doing so should not be minimized.

Second, there is a structural feature of negotiations between parties that are both unequal in power and deeply divided between moderates who are probably willing to compromise, but may be skeptical, and militants who are prepared to go to great lengths to sabotage any effort at diplomacy. Without implying precise parity, it is nonetheless true that both Israelis and Palestinians have been hesitant to make deals with counterparts who seem unwilling to discipline their own hard-liners. Israelis complain about the PLO's unwillingness to rein in the Hamas and Islamic Jihad extremists; Palestinians point to the unwillingness of Israeli governments to curb settlement activity in the occupied territories. Each side reads this as a sign that extremists are so strong that moderates are intimidated by them. Thus, why make concessions to moderates until they have shown their willingness to act against their own internal opposition? If this is a problem in the present, it also raises troubling questions about the future: Could a moderate leader who makes an agreement be replaced later on by an extremist? Would that mean that any agreement signed would unravel? These are questions that hang over most negotiations, but when leaders speak with broad backing and institutions are well established, it may be possible to allay some of these fears. Such conditions do not exist in the Arab-Israeli arena, where leadership is often quite personal and where opposition can be expressed in quite violent ways, sometimes with devastating consequences for diplomacy.

Third, in light of these structural realities and the intrinsic difficulty of finding solutions to many of the outstanding issues, the parties have become quite dependent on third-party mediation. Usually the United States has played this role, but not always with skill or success. Still, a pattern has developed since the negotiations of the mid-1970s, whereby each party tries to win the United States to its side, sometimes preferring that the United States put forward compromise positions rather than doing so themselves. Part of the game is to extract concessions from the third party during the ostensibly bilateral negotiations. Aid, promises of arms, and diplomatic support are all part of the common currency of endgame negotiations. Instead of the oft-cited "two-level" game, negotiations often resemble a three-level structure: each party has to deal with the home front, the adversary, and the United States at the same time. This puts a heavy responsibility on the third party to play its hand effectively. If it falters, the negotiations may be jeopardized.

While each of these factors played a part in the failure of the 1990s, the most vulnerable point on both sides, the element that inhibited the negotiators more than any other, seems to have been the weak domestic base of support of the leaders who were in charge of the negotiations. Time and again, they seem to have hesitated to make moves that might have advanced the negotiations for fear of losing domestic support. That, more than history or culture per se, more than the intrinsic difficulty of the issues, seems to have doomed the peace process of the 1990s. We turn now to the narrative of those events.

PLO Accepts 242 and Renounces Terrorism— December 1988

A crucial event that helped set the stage for the negotiations of the 1990s took place toward the end of 1987. In December of that year, Palestinians in the West Bank and Gaza began to engage in a sustained uprising against the Israeli occupation—the first intifada. Accompanied by strikes and civil disobedience, the intifada showed an impressive degree of politicization among Palestinians who had been living under Israeli occupation since 1967. For them—more than was the case for Palestinians in Lebanon or Jordan, for example—the issue was the occupation of the West Bank and Gaza, not Israel's existence per se.

The PLO, from its exile in Tunis, quickly sized up the new situation and sought to provide leadership for a movement that had caught it largely by surprise. One of the new elements in the intifada was the active role played by Islamist movements, especially Hamas, the only large Palestinian faction that was not affiliated with the PLO.

The intifada had at least two immediate consequences. First, it forced Israelis to question the wisdom of the policies that had led to the intifada. The right-wing government of Yitzhak Shamir had no strategy for peace and seemed to be mishandling a number of other issues as well, including relations with the United States. As the Soviet Union was falling apart, many new Jewish immigrants were arriving in Israel and their top priorities were economic—and the economy was not in good shape.

The second result of the intifada was that King Hussein of Jordan, long the preferred interlocutor on Palestinian affairs of Israelis and Americans alike, concluded that Jordan could no longer maintain its claim to the West Bank. The intifada, largely fueled by the energies of a younger generation for whom Jordan was a foreign country, convinced the king that he would be better off making clear to the world that Jordan was no longer the place for those who wanted to deal with the Palestinian issue. In an address in August 1988, he formally ended Jordan's administrative and legal ties to the West Bank and declared that henceforth the PLO would bear full responsibility for any negotiations on the Palestine issue.

Almost immediately an effort was made to see if the United States and the PLO might be ready to establish some form of relationship. The American conditions were conveyed clearly to the PLO: in return for the PLO's acceptance of UN Resolution 242, recognition of Israel's right to exist, and the renunciation of terrorism, the United States would be prepared to begin official talks with the PLO. In December 1988, after several months of maneuvering, Yasser Arafat finally uttered the magic words and the outgoing Reagan administration responded by agreeing to deal with the PLO. During the first year and a half of the new George H. W. Bush administration, official contacts took place between the PLO and a small number of American officials, especially in the American embassy in Tunis, until those talks were suspended in mid-1990.

Madrid—October 1991

The next step toward bringing the PLO into the diplomatic game took place in late 1991, after the Gulf War. President George H. W. Bush and his secretary of state, James Baker, worked to convene a peace conference between Israel and all its Arab neighbors. The issue arose, of course, of how and whether the Palestinians would be represented. Israeli prime minister Shamir was still unwilling to deal directly with the PLO, so a gimmick of sorts was devised. A joint Jordanian-Palestinian delegation was formed, with twice the number of delegates as all other national delegations, and the PLO agreed to select Palestinians for the delegation who would not come from the top ranks of the leadership and would not be known as residents of Jerusalem. Shamir could therefore say that he was not dealing with the PLO, while at the same time the PLO would clearly be calling the shots for its members of the combined Jordanian-Palestinian delegation. It was all a bit awkward, but it worked, and the PLO was therefore represented at the Madrid Conference.

Negotiations dragged on in a rather desultory fashion through 1992, with the Palestinian component of the joint Jordanian-Palestinian delegation acting increasingly on its own behalf. Israelis were becoming used to the idea of talking to Palestinians, even though Shamir still refused to acknowledge that he was dealing with the PLO. In early 1992, Shamir's internal position was weakened when President Bush, who, the previous fall, had signaled his reluctance to provide additional aid to Israel unless Shamir accepted a freeze on settlement activity, finally refused to provide $10 billion in loan guarantees because Shamir was unwilling to accept his conditions. Israelis went to the polls in mid-1992 and this time chose Yitzhak Rabin, a former general and former prime minister, a man with a reputation for toughness but with a pragmatic side as well.

The Oslo Accords—September 13, 1993

By the time Rabin became prime minister, Israelis had been living with the Palestinian intifada for almost five years. The costs to Israel of being an occupying power were becoming apparent in lives, money, and morale. At the same time, many new immigrants from the former Soviet Union were arriving in search of a better and more secure life. They were, on the whole, not strongly ideological and had little interest in the occupied territories.

Prime Minister Rabin, aided by his rival and colleague Shimon Peres, read the mood of fatigue that had settled over the Israelis and Palestinians and concluded that a new approach to peacemaking was needed. Breaking with the long-held preference for dealing with King Hussein of Jordan in any discussions of the West Bank, Rabin and Peres began to talk directly to the PLO through a secret channel provided by the Norwegians in early 1993. The result was the Oslo Accords of September 13, 1993, signed on the White House lawn in the presence of President Bill Clinton and sealed with the now-famous handshake between Rabin and Arafat.

The Oslo Accords and the accompanying exchange of letters did not settle all outstanding problems, but they did constitute a breakthrough in several regards. First, Israel and the PLO recognized each other. Henceforth it would be difficult for either to avoid direct dealings with the other. For Arafat, this constituted a long-sought step toward international legitimacy. On substantive issues, the Oslo Accords and the accompanying letters incorporated much of the Camp David approach, but with several innovations:

• First, at the outset of the interim period, the PLO would gain control of most of Gaza and the town of Jericho in the West Bank. In other words, there would be an initial territorial component of the agreement, with the promise of more as the interim period unfolded.

- Second, the accords included a provision for Palestinians to elect their own authority, with executive, legislative, and judicial powers (subject to agreement with Israel).

- Third, Palestinians, relying on informal discussions, understood that, with the exception of East Jerusalem and some natural expansion of existing settlements, Israel would no longer approve new settlements in the West Bank or Gaza and would remove financial incentives for Israelis to move there. But the text of the Oslo agreement made no explicit mention of this, and it remained a point of intense controversy.

- Fourth, the PLO would undertake to prevent armed attacks against Israel and to punish any perpetrators of violence against the Jewish state or Israeli citizens.

- Fifth, Israel would retain full control over settlements and roads linking them, as well as designated military outposts, during the transitional period.

- Finally, the two sides agreed that final-status talks would begin no later than two years from the start of the transitional period and would address "Jerusalem, refugees, settlements, security arrangements, borders, relations and cooperation with neighbors, and other issues of common interest."

The Oslo agreement also included a potentially crucial provision (Article IV), which stated, "Jurisdiction of the [elected Palestinian] Council will cover West Bank and Gaza Strip territory, except for issues that will be negotiated in the permanent status negotiations. The two sides view the West Bank and the Gaza Strip as a *single territorial unit,* whose integrity will be preserved during the interim period [emphasis added]." In short, Israel could not annex any of the territory during the interim period and the Palestinians could not declare statehood with full claims of sovereignty. This provision, however, did give the Palestinians some hope that they would be able to move toward statehood in most of the West Bank and Gaza by the end of the transitional period.

As with any agreement, the Oslo Accords could be variously interpreted and were not self-implementing. In fact, it was a fairly clear admission that even well-meaning moderate leaders could not confront the truly difficult issues of Jerusalem, settlements, refugees, borders, and final security arrangements without a cooling-off period. The hope among those who advocated the Oslo approach was that time would work in favor of compromise; that confidence would be gained as practical solutions were found for vexing problems; and that both sides would develop a stake in the new arrangements that would provide an impetus for tackling the final-status issues a few years down the road. Both parties needed time, it was argued, to prepare their publics. Whether that time would be available was uncertain.

Agreement on the Gaza Strip and the Jericho Area— May 4, 1994

The Oslo Accords were little more than a general framework of principles. Much remained to be fleshed out before the interim period would actually begin. In fact, eight months of arduous negotiations were required to work out the practical measures governing Palestinian elections, security, the initial withdrawal, and the extent of authority that would actually be transferred to the Palestinians. Signed in Cairo in May 1994, this agreement finally started the clock ticking in terms of subsequent steps to be carried out during the interim period. For example, final-status talks were to begin no later than May 4, 1996, and the interim period should end by May 4, 1999.

This agreement, while more precise than its predecessor, mainly dealt with the initial phase of the interim period. Many details remained to be worked out. But now, at least, a foundation had been laid; Arafat and his colleagues had returned to Gaza; and a new dynamic in Israeli-Palestinian relations seemed possible.

Oslo II—September 28, 1995

By this phase in the peace process, Rabin and Arafat were beginning to treat each other as partners. Both were facing elections in 1996, and the Oslo II agreement was, in part, designed to meet the political needs of each side. For Arafat, the agreement held out the prospect that Israeli troops would leave all but one of the major towns of the West Bank—Hebron was the exception—shortly before Palestinian elections. Even Hebron would come under Palestinian authority soon thereafter, with special arrangements in place to guard the small community of Jewish zealots who had settled in the old city near the Ibrahimi Mosque/Tomb of the Patriarchs. And over the next year, if all went well, three further withdrawals would take place that, in the view of the Palestinians, would leave them in charge of some 75 percent of the territory of the West Bank and Gaza and virtually all of its Arab population.

Even on the sensitive issue of Jerusalem, Arafat could point to a symbolic breakthrough. In the elections for the Palestinian Authority, Palestinian residents of Jerusalem would be able to vote, although the procedures would be slightly different than elsewhere in the West Bank. Most Palestinians living in East Jerusalem would cast their ballots beyond the city limits, but a small number would actually vote within the city limits. For the Palestinians, this was an important gesture, showing that Jerusalem's political status was not completely settled by the unilateral act of Israeli annexation.

For Rabin and the Israeli peace camp, Oslo II also contained some positive elements. After Palestinian elections had been held, the new Palestinian Council would revoke those elements of the Palestine National Charter that called for Israel's destruction. In addition, Arafat explicitly accepted that "Israelis and Settlements" would remain exclusively under Israeli control for the duration of the interim period. And he undertook to prevent attacks on Israelis from territory under his control. Increasingly, the Israelis were drawing Arafat into a neighborly relationship, forcing him to concentrate on the immediate needs of his new constituents in the West Bank and Gaza at the expense of the more militant Palestinian diaspora. In this new role, Arafat, it was hoped, could be expected to understand why it was in his own self-interest to help Israel police his own radical wing.

The security provisions of Oslo II were far-reaching and left Israel in charge of what was termed "external security, as well as the responsibility for overall security of Israelis for the purpose of safeguarding their internal security and public order." The West Bank and Gaza were divided into three security zones. In Zone A, including most of the urban areas, the Palestinian Authority would be in charge; in Zone B, the surrounding rural areas, Palestinians and Israelis would share security responsibilities at the outset, but gradually Israeli forces would withdraw in three stages, at six-month intervals, over an eighteen-month period. The precise stages of withdrawal were not specified, but it was understood that at the end of the period the Palestinians would be in charge of about 75 percent of the West Bank and Gaza. This would leave Israel in charge of Zone C, where the Israeli settlers lived, and in control of roads leading to and from the settlements and military installations.

Finally, the agreement spelled out the jurisdiction of the new Palestinian Authority. In brief, the Palestinian Council had responsibility in those areas explicitly ceded by the Israelis, but excluding "issues that will be negotiated in the permanent-status negotiations: Jerusalem, settlements, specified military locations, Palestinian refugees, borders, foreign relations and Israelis."

According to an optimistic scenario widely held at the time, the Oslo II Accord would set the stage for a mutually reinforcing set of developments: Israeli troops would leave most Palestinian cities and towns; Arafat and his supporters would win free elections, thereby acquiring legitimacy for the next phase of the negotiations; the Palestinian Council would revoke the offensive clauses of the National Charter; Rabin and Peres would soundly defeat their rivals at the polls; the agreement on Israeli withdrawal from Hebron would be implemented; the final-status talks would begin in earnest; another phase of withdrawal would take place from portions of Zones B and C in September 1996, again in March 1997, and a final phase in September 1997. By then, the Palestinians would, in many ways, be effectively running their own lives and the final-status negotiations would proceed to establish the borders of a more or less independent Palestinian state.

But this, of course, was not to be. Rabin was assassinated by a Jewish extremist in November 1995; a spate of terror attacks in February and March 1996 killed nearly sixty Israelis; negotiations with Syria were suspended; Israeli troops launched harsh retaliatory raids into Lebanon in spring 1996, alienating significant numbers of Palestinian Israelis who might have otherwise voted for Peres; Netanyahu narrowly defeated Peres at the polls in May 1996; the Hebron agreement and the first phase of withdrawal from Zone B were halted by the Likud-led government; and in September 1996, armed Israelis and Palestinians clashed in some of the worst violence to date. By early 1997, the peace process was in deep trouble.

Beilin–Abu Mazen Understanding

The closest that Israelis and Palestinians came in the 1990s to bridging the gaps between them was in talks that took place from late 1995 until early 1996. Peres's aide Yossi Beilin met frequently in secret with PLO leader Mahmud Abbas (Abu Mazen) and the two came close to reaching compromise agreements on many final-status issues. According to Beilin's account:

> Israel would recognize a demilitarized Palestinian state with all the attributes of sovereignty. Israel would annex a portion of the West Bank along the 1967 lines that would thereby incorporate many settlements and the large majority of Israeli settlers (approximately 100,000 of the 140,000) under full Israeli sovereignty; these settlements would be as Israeli as Tel Aviv and Beersheba. The annexation would come in the framework of an exchange of territories, in which Israel's narrow waist would be widened and the Palestinians would receive extra territory along the Gaza Strip. Israeli settlers not annexed to Israel would have the option of compensation or living in the Palestinian state, with special security arrangements for them. As for refugees, none would return to Israeli territory but there would be no limitation on immigration to the Palestinian state.[1]

Jerusalem was the toughest issue of all. There Beilin and Abu Mazen reached a tentative understanding as follows: Palestinians would recognize West Jerusalem as sovereign Israeli territory and Israel's capital, bringing world recognition of West Jerusalem as Israel's capital. For Palestinians, the geographic area of "al-Quds" is in fact much larger than the municipal boundaries of Israeli Jerusalem. Therefore, Israel would recognize a Palestinian capital in "al-Quds" that would actually be in an area like Abu Dis, currently a Jerusalem suburb. East Jerusalem would be designated by both parties as disputed territory with the status quo remaining in place for the indefinite future; Israel would still operate there as de facto sovereign but not recognized as such. The Palestinians would have extraterritorial status over the Haram al-Sharif (the Temple Mount), which essentially mirrors the current situation, in which the Islamic authorities control the site. The city of Jerusalem itself would be divided into boroughs, with each borough (e.g., Arab, ultraorthodox Jewish Israeli, secular Israeli) enjoying significant autonomy under a "roof municipality." Arab residents within Israeli borders could be citizens of the Palestinian state.[2]

The Hebron Agreement—January 15, 1997

As part of the Oslo II agreement, Israel agreed to withdraw from all the major cities and towns of the West Bank, including Hebron. The actual redeployment of Israeli troops from 80 percent of Hebron was delayed by mutual agreement, however, because of the special problems involving the small group of militant Israeli settlers located near the city's holy sites. The Palestinians agreed that the pullout, originally scheduled for March 1996, could be delayed until after Israeli elections. Then, when Netanyahu became prime minister, he insisted on renegotiating the Hebron agreement, arguing that its security provisions were inadequate.

Hebron demonstrates graphically the problems of trying to provide security for both communities when they are in close proximity. To protect some four to five hundred Israelis living within the city, the Israeli army demanded a substantial presence in the city, plus strict limits on Palestinian security forces. To protect the Israelis in the city center, Israel would keep control of about 20 percent of the city, including some thirty thousand Palestinian residents. Israel also sought the right of hot pursuit, but eventually dropped this demand in the face of firm Palestinian rejection. Israel also demanded exclusive guardianship over the Tomb of the Patriarchs, which is located within the Ibrahimi Mosque. The Palestinians strongly resented the way in which Netanyahu abrogated an agreement already entered into by the Labor government and were able to rebuff some of his demands for changes in the protocols. During the last half of 1996, endless discussions, often involving intense American mediation, were held in order to resolve this dispute. A revised agreement was finally reached on January 15, 1997.

Apart from the intrinsic difficulty of resolving the problems of Hebron, the delay in the negotiations was due to the fact that Arafat was trying to ensure that other issues that had been agreed upon with Labor would not be jettisoned in the same way as the Hebron agreement. Once Netanyahu reopened the Hebron accord, Arafat felt justified in trying to pin down the understanding reached with Labor on subsequent stages of withdrawal. As of September 1996, Israel was to have made a significant withdrawal from Zone B. That did not happen. Another withdrawal was to take place in March 1997 and another in September 1997. Comments by Netanyahu and his colleagues had raised doubts as to whether any of these further withdrawals would be made. Those Israelis who opposed the withdrawals had argued that Arafat had violated terms of Oslo II and therefore Israel was relieved of its obligations under the agreement.

Netanyahu gave credence to the view that he did not intend to make further withdrawals by proposing that the parties move directly to the final-status issues without any intermediate withdrawals taking place. While this sounded reasonable to some observers, it would ensure that the final-status issues would be addressed from a much different starting point than if Israel were to carry out the scheduled redeployments. Not surprisingly, Arafat wanted to enter the final-status talks with as much territory already under his control as possible. So the argument over Hebron, like so many issues in dispute, was part of a larger set of concerns about the eventual shape of peace between Israel and the Palestinians. At each stage of negotiations, precedents were being set and seeming side issues worked their way into the forefront of the discussions.

When the negotiations on Hebron were concluded in mid-January, Netanyahu and Arafat had agreed upon a revised schedule of withdrawals from Zones B and C. Instead of completing the redeployment by September 1997, Israel would be given until August 1998 to carry out the three-stage withdrawal. The missing piece in the agreement, however, was still the extent of the withdrawals. Netanyahu insisted, and the American mediators concurred, that the extent of these withdrawals would be determined exclusively by Israel. Palestinians insisted that they should have a voice in how much territory would be relinquished.

Optimists argued that Netanyahu's willingness to negotiate any withdrawal at all with the PLO showed a welcome turn toward realism. Some maintained that he was wedded to the peace process as conceived by Labor. But there was little in the Hebron Agreement per se that lent support to such an interpretation. After all, Netanyahu did little more than agree to carry out a commitment already entered into by his predecessor, while winning for himself more time to decide on additional withdrawals. Nothing in the agreement specified how much additional territory Israel would evacuate in the subsequent three stages. Nor did it say anything about the substance of the other outstanding issues, or the final-status negotiations, which were scheduled to begin immediately.

The Wye River Negotiations—October 1998

For most of the next two years, 1997 and 1998, negotiations remained almost at a standstill. This was a frustrating period for both sides. Israelis argued that Palestinians were not taking their security responsibilities seriously, that they had violated many terms of the Oslo agreement, and that Israel would take no further steps on withdrawal in the absence of reciprocity. All of this was consistent with Netanyahu's known skepticism about Oslo and distaste for giving up any additional territory in the West Bank.

On the Palestinian side, the frustrations were also numerous. First, the promised second and third phases of withdrawal were long overdue and Netanyahu had made clear that they would not in any case involve much territory. In addition, settlements were continuing to expand and Palestinian land was being expropriated as new roads were being built to link up the settlements in the West Bank. Overall, the Palestinian standard of living had probably deteriorated since Oslo, and certainly many aspects of everyday life, such as movement from one area of the West Bank to another, had become more difficult. Arafat's critics were openly saying that Oslo had proved to be a trap.

President Clinton began to show signs of frustration with the stalled negotiations and by early 1998 was pressing for a clear Israeli commitment to withdrawal from an additional 13 percent of the occupied Palestinian territories. Taking a page from Jimmy Carter's book, Clinton finally called for a summit meeting in October 1998 at the Wye River Plantation outside Washington, DC The talks were difficult and Clinton's engagement was episodic, but in the end a deal was struck. Once again, some optimists began to say that only a hard-line Israeli prime minister could really negotiate territorial concessions with the Palestinians. But after a very small withdrawal in the northern part of the West Bank, Israel dug in its heels and refused to go further, arguing that the Palestinians were still not living up to their responsibilities. By this time, Netanyahu was in deep political trouble at home, and his strained relations with Clinton were not helping much.

The End of the Five-Year Transition and Barak's Election as Prime Minister

The spring of 1999 proved to be a momentous period for Israeli-Palestinian peacemaking. According to the Oslo timetable, the transitional period was supposed to be reaching its end in May 1999. Of course, the agreement had not said what would happen if the parties had still not concluded the negotiations. For the Palestinians, there was a sense that they had waited long enough and the appropriate next step was a unilateral declaration of independence. The Israelis made clear that they would view this as a violation of Oslo and would respond harshly.

In this tense atmosphere, with forebodings of possible violence on the horizon, Israelis went to the polls and decisively rejected Netanyahu in favor of Ehud Barak, a protégé of Rabin's who presented himself as embodying the same combination of toughness and pragmatism as his mentor. Barak was frequently described as "brilliant," and he seemed to have little patience for those who did not see things his way. He also was quite new to the political arena. Nonetheless, he represented a fresh approach to peace talks and both Arafat and Clinton were encouraged by his election.

Barak had campaigned on a platform promising that Israeli troops in south Lebanon would be withdrawn within a year. This led him to a lengthy and ultimately unsuccessful effort to reach an understanding with Syria. Not for the first time, the Israeli desire for a deal with Syria— strategically important, seemingly "doable," and possibly not too controversial on the domestic front—got in the way of the more complex, but also more urgent, Palestinian talks. As a result, during much of his first year, Barak ignored Arafat and the mounting evidence of Palestinian frustration. Also, belying his reputation for moderation, he refused to carry out the withdrawals that had been agreed upon in the Wye River Accord. From his perspective, it would cost him politically to make additional interim withdrawals and he would be better off preserving his political capital for one big comprehensive effort to reach a final agreement with Arafat. As a result, Arafat became highly suspicious of Barak's intentions and began to see his own popular support erode in favor of the more radical Hamas movement. It is impossible to understand what happened next without paying attention to the complex interactions among three complex personalities—Barak, Arafat, and Clinton.

The Stockholm Talks

It was not until spring 2000 that Barak reached the conclusion that the search for an agreement with Syria was not going to work. Clinton had conveyed the Israeli position to President Hafiz al-Asad and the Syrian leader had turned it down. Barak nonetheless decided to go ahead with the promised withdrawal of Israeli troops from Lebanon, and then he finally turned his attention to the Palestinian track. Almost immediately, some Palestinians pointed out that the Lebanese militants, by using violence, had managed to get the Israelis to make a complete withdrawal from Lebanon. Why, some Palestinians said, should they not follow suit? Negotiations had produced little. Maybe it was time for a second and more aggressive intifada.

Despite mounting tensions, a promising phase of resumed diplomacy took place in secret talks near Stockholm. For the first time since the Abu Mazen–Beilin talks, the two sides began to engage seriously with all of the hard issues of the final-status agreement except for Jerusalem. They discussed refugees, borders and settlements, security, and statehood. A draft agreement was developed, with each side's positions spelled out. But word soon leaked that the talks were taking place and that Israel was considering matters that were highly sensitive for Israeli public opinion. Barak, who in any case felt that only he could make the final deal, decided to suspend these talks. In their place, he proposed to Clinton that a summit meeting of the three leaders be held. But he was unwilling to tell the Americans how far he was willing to go at such a summit. They had to take it on faith that he would be ready to make the concessions necessary to reach an agreement.

Arafat was skeptical. He had forged a fairly good relationship with Clinton by this time, but he was still unsure about Barak. He told Clinton explicitly that the parties needed more time to prepare for a summit, that at least several more weeks of secret talks were essential. He said that he feared that a summit might fail to resolve all the issues, that he would inevitably be blamed for the failure, and that it would be extremely hard to then resume momentum in the negotiations. Clinton, however, was ever sensitive to Barak's political timetable, and to his own political calendar —the U.S. presidential campaign would go into high gear in September, and although he could not run, his vice president would be in the race and his wife would be running for senator of New York. Thus, if progress were to be made, it should preferably be right away, at least in terms of Israeli and American political needs. For Arafat, in contrast, it was more important that the final deal be one that could be sold to the skeptical Palestinian public, and if it took a bit longer to reach that agreement, it was no problem for him. He had no elections to worry about, after all.

Camp David II

In mid-July 2000, President Clinton convened a summit meeting of Barak and Arafat at Camp David. Arafat had been reluctant to attend, fearing that the talks might fail and that he would be blamed. Barak, however, was convinced that further talks at a lower level would be a waste of time, and, for him, time was of the essence, since his popular support was eroding. Clinton also felt the pressure of time as his mandate was coming to an end.

According to most accounts, Barak and Arafat did not interact very much at the summit. Instead, Barak submitted his positions to Clinton, who then conveyed them to a remarkably passive and unresponsive Arafat. Barak did offer to withdraw conditionally from some 90 percent of the West Bank and Gaza; there were serious discussions, but no agreement, about refugees and Jerusalem; and Israel seemed prepared to accept the idea of an independent Palestinian state, provided it remained essentially demilitarized. There were also discussions of long-term leases of land, land swaps, and consolidation of settlements along the new border. The issue that could not be solved in the time available was sovereignty over the Haram al-Sharif/Temple Mount area in Jerusalem. Barak offered a form of Palestinian "custodianship," but Arafat insisted on "sovereignty." After some two weeks of negotiations, the talks ended in failure, and Clinton made it clear that he thought Arafat was more to blame than Barak.

The Clinton Proposals

Despite the collapse of talks at Camp David, efforts were soon made to re-open channels between the two parties. Barak and Arafat even met again in late September. But domestic politics on both sides immediately intruded. Likud party leader Ariel Sharon insisted on visiting the Haram al-Sharif/Temple Mount area; Palestinians reacted violently, and within days Israelis and Palestinians were locked into a new round of violence. The second intifada had begun. Israelis suspected that Arafat had ordered the attacks in order to pressure Israel for more concessions. Palestinians saw the intifada as the natural response of an occupied people to deteriorating circumstances in their everyday lives, a reaction to provocations and humiliations at the hands of Israelis, and the right of any oppressed people to resist.

Soon Barak was pressured to call new elections, and, with time running extremely short, Clinton finally put forward American ideas on

December 23, 2000. In many ways, the suggested compromises looked quite balanced. Both sides were able to point to significant points in their favor, but there were also ambiguities and unresolved issues. Israel, according to Clinton, would withdraw from about 95 percent of the Palestinian land occupied in 1967, and land swaps would give the Palestinians another 2 or 3 percent; Jerusalem would be divided, with Israel keeping the Jewish quarter but relinquishing control of the Haram al-Sharif/Temple Mount area. Palestinian refugees would be given a number of choices involving compensation and some form of "return," while making it clear that the basic demography of Israel would not be affected by the outcome.

Barak, by now almost certain to lose the election scheduled for February 2001, gave his hesitant and conditional support to the Clinton proposals. In his only meeting with Clinton about the plan, on January 2, 2001, Arafat said that he also accepted the proposals in principle but had some reservations. One concerned the Western Wall of the Temple Mount complex. He was willing to grant Israel sovereignty over the so-called Wailing Wall, the exposed part of the Western Wall that adjoined the Jewish quarter, but not the entire Western Wall, which extended some fifty meters into the Muslim quarter. Second, he would not accept that Israel could use Palestinian airspace. Finally, he simply said that a new formula on refugees would have to be found. Clinton and U.S. mediator Dennis Ross decided that these reservations went beyond the "parameters" of what had to be accepted, and they therefore concluded that there was no hope for a deal.[3]

Taba Finale

A last-ditch effort to reach agreement was made in late January at the Egyptian resort town of Taba. Israeli negotiators, working without much support from Barak, fleshed out details of the map that they might be prepared to accept. Further discussions took place on how refugees might actually express their choices. At times the mood was hopeful, as tough issues were seriously addressed by negotiators who had come to know each other well and felt a common commitment to making every effort for peace. But it was too little, too late. Ariel Sharon overwhelmingly defeated Barak in the February election, and with the change of government the peace process came to a halt, at least for the time being.

Conclusion

Sharon was elected as "Mr. Security," the man who would end the second intifada and teach the Palestinians a lesson in political realism. Sharon had a negative view of Arafat and felt that he could not be a partner in peace talks. He was known as a hard-liner, but with less of an ideological outlook than some Likud purists. Still, no one expected the architect of Israel's settlement expansion policies of the 1980s to be particularly interested in territorial concessions.

In fact, the period 2001–3 was particularly violent and the parties did not succeed in resuming serious negotiations. Instead, Israel reoccupied much of the West Bank after a series of suicide bombings in early 2002. Meanwhile, the administration of George W. Bush gave significant backing to Sharon's campaign to delegitimize and even unseat—but not to physically eliminate or exile—Arafat.

By early 2003, there was slight movement on the diplomatic front, as both sides seemed tired of the unending violence. A so-called Roadmap to peace was put forward with the support of the United States, Russia, the European Union, and the UN secretary-general. In March 2003, in the aftermath of the war in Iraq, an effort was under way to empower a new Palestinian prime minister, Mahmud Abbas (Abu Mazen), and to bring about an end to the violence. But neither side was willing to carry out its obligations under the Roadmap, so by the end of 2003 the chances of success for this most recent diplomatic effort looked slim. Indeed, Sharon began to talk of unilateral pullbacks to a line that would be determined exclusively by Israel, presumably in the vicinity of the security barrier that was being rapidly built.

The strange part of this dismal story is that majorities of both Israelis and Palestinians still seemed prepared for peace and understood that painful concessions would be needed. The idea of a Palestinian state was no longer particularly controversial. In fact, in late 2003 private initiatives by Israelis and Palestinians produced an outline of a final agreement and a related set of principles that won wide endorsement, especially from members of the international community. But the leaders on both sides of the conflict seemed incapable of leading their publics to these types of compromises. And yet no alternative credible framework has been developed by either party.

In conclusion, this chapter has tried to identify the range of reasons that have been offered for the failure of the sustained efforts to negotiate an end to the Israeli-Palestinian conflict in the 1990s. The weight of historical legacies and cultural sensitivities was noted, particularly for the way in which they shape public attitudes that may constrain negotiators, along with more structural features of the conflict, such as the asymmetry of power between the disputants, the embeddedness of this conflict in a web of other international issues, the dependency on the mediating role of the United States, the role of key personalities, and the intrinsic complexity of the problems that separate them. Despite these apparent obstacles, the parties actually came quite close to agreement on many of the key issues, and this may be a reason to hope that eventually negotiations may resume with some chance of success. If negotiators are ever going to reach an agreement, they will have to find a way to bring their often-skeptical publics with them. If there was a significant failure in the 1990s, it was the inability or the unwillingness of any of the major political figures to prepare Israelis and Palestinians for the trade-offs that might be needed to bring this conflict to an end.

Notes

1. Yossi Beilin, "Special Policy Report to the Washington Institute for Near East Policy," *Peacewatch,* no. 112 (1996): 2. For the text of the Abu Mazen–Beilin framework agreement, see http://www.brookings.edu/dybdocroot/press/appendix/appen_t.htm.

2. Ibid.

3. Dennis Ross, *The Missing Piece: The Inside Story of the Fight for Middle East Peace* (New York: Farrar, Strauss and Giroux, 2004), 10–14, 755–756.

Bibliography

Barzilai, Amnon. "A Brief History of the Missed Opportunity." *Ha'aretz,* June 5, 2002.

———. "EU Description of the Outcome of Permanent Status Talks at Taba." *Ha'aretz,* February 16, 2002.

Beilin, Yossi. *The Path to Geneva: The Quest for a Permanent Agreement, 1996–2004.* New York: RDV Books, 2004.

Enderlin, Charles. *Shattered Dreams: The Failure of the Peace Process in the Middle East, 1995–2002.* New York: Other Press, 2002.

Haniyah, Akram. "Camp David Diary," *al-Ayyam* (Arabic), translated in FBIS–Near East/South Asia, part one, July 29, 2000.

Hirsh, Michael. "Blowing the Best Chance." *Newsweek,* April 1, 2002.

Klein, Menachem. "The Origins of Intifada II and Rescuing Peace for Israelis and Palestinians." Lecture, Foundation for Middle East Peace and Middle East Institute, Washington, DC, October 2, 2002.

Lustick, Ian S. "Ending Protracted Conflicts: The Oslo Peace Process between Political Partnership and Legality." *Cornell International Law Journal* 30, no. 3 (1997).

Makovsky, David. "Taba Mythchief." *National Interest* (Spring 2003).

Malley, Robert. "Fictions about the Failure at Camp David." *New York Times,* July 8, 2001.

Malley, Robert, and Hussein Agha. "A Tragedy of Errors." *New York Review of Books,* August 9, 2001.

Morris, Benny. "Camp David and After: An Exchange. 1. An Interview with Ehud Barak." *New York Review of Books,* June 13, 2002.

Pundak, Ron. "From Oslo to Taba: What Went Wrong?" *Survival* 43, no. 3 (Autumn 2001).

Quandt, William B. *Peace Process: American Diplomacy and the Arab-Israeli Conflict since 1967.* Washington, DC: Brookings, 2001.

Ross, Dennis. "From Oslo to Camp David to Taba: Setting the Record Straight." Panel interview with Margaret Warner, Jim Hoagland, and Robert Satloff at the Washington Institute for Near East Policy, Washington, DC, August 8, 2001.

———. *The Missing Piece: The Inside Story of the Fight for Middle East Peace.* New York: Farrar, Strauss and Giroux, 2004.

———. "Think Again: Yasir Arafat." *Foreign Policy* (July-August 2002).

Ross, Dennis, and Gidi Grinstein. Reply to Hussein Agha and Robert Malley. "Camp David: An Exchange." *New York Review of Books,* September 20, 2001.

Rubenstein, Danny. "It's Time to Learn the Lesson." *Ha'aretz,* September 9, 2002.

Sher, Gilead. *The Brink of Peace?* Special Report on the Arab-Israeli Peace Process, no. 318. Washington, DC: Washington Institute for Near East Policy, April 18, 2001.

Sommer, Allison Kaplan. "U.S. Ambassador: Oslo Failed due to Lack of U.S. Involvement." *Jerusalem Post,* December 7, 2001.

Sontag, Deborah. "Quest for Mideast Peace: How and Why It Failed." *New York Times,* July 26, 2001.

Steinberg, Gerald. "Conflict Management and Negotiation." Seminar: Options for Israeli-Palestinian Negotiations after Oslo, Bar Ilan University, December 6, 2000.

3

Surviving Opportunities

❖❖❖❖❖❖❖❖❖❖❖❖❖❖❖❖❖❖❖❖❖❖❖❖❖❖❖❖❖❖❖❖❖❖❖❖

Palestinian Negotiating Patterns in

❖❖❖❖❖❖❖❖❖❖❖❖❖❖❖❖❖❖❖❖❖❖❖❖❖❖❖❖❖❖❖❖❖❖❖❖

Peace Talks with Israel

❖❖❖❖❖❖❖❖❖❖❖❖❖❖❖❖❖❖❖❖❖❖❖❖❖

Omar M. Dajani

In the months following the Middle East peace summit at Camp David in July 2000, an unflattering image of Palestinian negotiators began to take hold in the international media. A chorus of public officials, political commentators, and journalists resurrected the phrase, coined by the late Israeli diplomat Abba Eban more than three decades earlier, that appeared to capture so aptly the Palestinian approach to international diplomacy: "The Palestinians never miss an opportunity to miss an opportunity," they repeated, linking Palestine Liberation Organization (PLO) chairman Yasser Arafat's[1] refusal to accept the peace terms offered by Israel's then prime minister Ehud Barak to the chain of other historic moments and "generous" offers the Palestinians had allowed to pass—the 1937 Peel Commission Report, the 1939 White Paper, the 1947 United Nations Partition Plan, and the 1978 Camp David Accords. The implication was clear: the Palestinian leadership remained unreliable and constitutionally incapable of compromise, lost in a dream world of revolutionary slogans and UN resolutions—in sum, unequal to the role that history had repeatedly offered them as partners in a peaceful settlement in the Middle East.

A full picture of the events at Camp David would emerge only later. Subsequent accounts revealed that other factors were at play: the two sides had prepared insufficiently, not even having discussed some of the most contentious issues prior to the summit; the U.S. team was disorganized, rent by internal divisions, and inattentive to both Palestinian interests and the concerns of the broader Arab and Islamic worlds; and the terms of Prime Minister Barak's "generous offer" to the Palestinians were neither generous nor presented coherently as an offer.[2] More than a year after the Camp David summit, a member of the U.S. peace team observed that "paradoxically, this tragedy of errors contains a message of hope. For it points to the possibility that things can turn out differently if they are done differently."[3]

Indeed, by the close of negotiations in January 2001, the gaps between the two sides' positions had narrowed considerably. In a lecture given in August 2003, Gilead Sher, Israel's chief negotiator during that period, expressed the view that it had been possible to reach a reasonable Palestinian-Israeli agreement within a reasonable time frame,[4] an assessment shared by senior Palestinian negotiator Saeb Ereikat, who remarked, also in August 2003, that if negotiators on both sides were given a mandate to make peace, they required only "six weeks of drafting" to conclude an agreement.[5]

The fact that the peace talks came so close to yielding an agreement, but ultimately failed to do so, is both an indictment of the negotiations process —and the parties' approaches to it—and an injunction to ensure that future talks achieve better results. With that end in mind, this chapter examines the ways Palestinians negotiated with Israelis during the Oslo process from 1993 to 2001, focusing on the permanent-status negotiations held at the end of that period. To be sure, Palestinian negotiating behavior is neither singular in style nor the inevitable consequence of Palestinian history. Nevertheless, the combined experiences of statelessness, dispossession, disenfranchisement, and exile, reinforced at each stage of Palestinian history, did present Palestinians with a double bind: they raised their expectations regarding the requirements for a just peace settlement and, at the same time, denied them the tools they needed to achieve their goals— above all, an institutionally coherent government with the authority to address its people's needs and a stable national space within which to test (and temper) their political ideals. These liabilities did much to shape the priorities and conduct of Palestinian negotiators during the Oslo process. On the one hand, negotiators sought a clean break from arrangements that had prevented Palestinians from controlling their lives in the past and sought to level the playing field by introducing international law and third parties into the negotiations. On the other hand, their efforts to achieve these goals were undermined by their own political disorganization, fierce internal competition, and lack of domestic political legitimacy. Ultimately, as discussed below, Israeli negotiating behavior reinforced these patterns, rather than compensating for them, contributing to the misattribution of motives by both parties and deepening mutual distrust.

This chapter begins by identifying key factors that have shaped the Palestinian approach to negotiations, including Palestinian history, political organization, and religious and ethnic affiliations. The second section of the chapter reviews the salient patterns of Palestinian negotiating behavior during the peace talks: the Palestinians' overall approach, how they assembled teams and prepared for negotiations, and the ways in which they tended to use compromise, language, law, pressure, and public opinion in the talks. The third and final section examines the ways in which Palestinian-Israeli negotiating dynamics contributed to the parties' failure to conclude a peace deal.

Factors Shaping Palestinian Negotiating Behavior

Cross-cultural negotiations theory postulates that a nation's experience shapes its diplomatic culture and negotiating style—the meanings attached to words, the motives attributed to adversaries, the concepts of what is permissible and what is insulting.[6] In the Palestinian case, however, a "national" experience is as difficult to define as it has been to achieve. Of course, no national experience is uniform, but the Palestinian experience has been particularly—even characteristically—varied. As Edward Said writes, "Our characteristic mode is not a narrative in which scenes take place *seriatim*, but rather broken narratives, fragmentary compositions, and self-consciously staged testimonials, in which the narrative voice keeps stumbling over itself, its obligations, and its limitations."[7] The experiences of dispossession, exile, and military occupation have deprived Palestinians not only of the experience of living together as a nation but also of the opportunity to build a unified national narrative and tradition. Palestinian historian Rashid Khalidi observes, "The Frenchwoman would refer her identity in some measure to a powerful, generations-old 'historical' narrative of Frenchness, propagated with authority since some time in the nineteenth century by a unified school system and other means at the disposal of the French state. In contrast, given the lack of such a state or such a unified educational system, the Palestinian would be more likely to refer identity to a number of 'historical' narratives, each carrying a different valence and a somewhat different message."[8] Accordingly, it is difficult to point to a single shared narrative that explains Palestinian negotiating behavior or to plot with any precision the consequences, sometimes decades later, of a given set of experiences.

With these caveats in mind, this section reviews some of the central strands of Palestinian experience, examining the key historical, political, religious, and regional factors that have shaped Palestinian negotiating culture.

Historical Experience

Palestinian history is marked by three major milestones: the *nakba* ("catastrophe") of 1948, Israel's military occupation of the West Bank and Gaza Strip, and Palestinian interim self-government under the Oslo Accords. These experiences, elements of which have been mutually reinforcing, have had an enduring effect on how Palestinians negotiate and on what their substantive priorities are.

The Nakba

The *nakba* is the experience that has perhaps most defined Palestinian history. For Palestinians, it is not merely a political event—the establishment of the state of Israel on 78 percent of the territory of the Palestine Mandate—or even, primarily, a humanitarian one—the creation of the modern world's most enduring refugee problem. The *nakba* is of existential significance to Palestinians, representing both the shattering of the Palestinian community in Palestine and the consolidation of a shared national consciousness. In the words of Baruch Kimmerling and Joel Migdal, "Between the last month of 1947 and the first four and a half months of 1948, the Palestinian Arab community would *cease to exist* as a social and political entity."[9] Hundreds of villages would be destroyed, urban life in Palestine's most populous Arab communities would disappear, and almost a million Palestinians would be rendered homeless and/or stateless.

At the same time, "the shared events of 1948 . . . brought the Palestinians closer together in terms of their collective consciousness, even as they were physically dispersed all over the Middle East and beyond."[10] To some extent, dispossession erased gaps between urban and rural, well-to-do and poor, and literate and illiterate, Palestinians in many countries facing myriad restrictions on their political and economic opportunities, irrespective of their previous station or lot in life in Palestine.[11] Although it bears emphasizing that the Palestinian national movement predated the *nakba* by several decades, and many Palestinians' sense of connection to their towns and lands extends back many generations further,[12] it seems clear that nothing forged Palestinian identity so surely as the loss of Palestine.

The centrality of the *nakba* to Palestinian identity formation would later affect both the substance and the style of Palestinian negotiations. The first major consequence would be the close association of Palestinianness with statelessness, with all of its practical consequences: lack of control over where one goes—or stays—lack of clarity on rights and status (or worse, express restrictions on political and civil rights), and permanent insecurity. Palestinian political scientist Yezid Sayigh observes, "Palestinianism was a natural response to *al-nakba,* but it was the experience of social and political marginality that effectively transformed it from a 'popular grass-roots patriotism' into a proto-nationalism in the decade after 1948."[13] Describing how the experience of marginality manifested itself in Palestinians' identity, Khalidi writes, "The quintessential Palestinian experience, which illustrates some of the most basic issues raised by Palestinian identity, takes place at a border, an airport, a checkpoint: in short, at any one of those many modern barriers where identities are checked and verified. . . . For it is at these borders and barriers that the six million Palestinians are singled out for 'special treatment,' and are forcefully reminded of their identity."[14] This experience would generate great sensitivity on the part of Palestinian negotiators to demands for external control over Palestinian borders (and movement, in general) and over determinations of who would be entitled to citizenship in the new state, as well as a desire for national symbols, from postage stamps to a "presidency" to national armed forces.

Second, the *nakba* reinforced the centrality of land in the Palestinian-Israeli conflict. In his memoir, *I Saw Ramallah,* Palestinian poet Mourid Barghouthi recalls asking himself, upon crossing the Jordan River after a lengthy period of exile, "What is so special about [the land of Palestine], except that we have lost it?"[15] To be sure, the issue of land was central to the conflict decades before the *nakba:* Palestinian opposition to land sales by absentee landlords to Jewish settlers "cement[ed] the link between members of the Palestinian elite who opposed Zionism on grounds of principle, and the *fellahin* (peasantry) whose resistance caught the popular imagination and thereby played a vital role in mobilizing opinion both in Palestine and the Arab world."[16] The *nakba,* however, made land even more significant, not only affecting a far greater number of Palestinians, but also creating widespread social uprootedness and depriving refugees of the social status that land ownership had conferred.[17] This centrality of title to and control over land (and related resources such as water), reinforced again by the experience of occupation, would later constrain Palestinian negotiators' consideration of further cession of territory to Israel.

Third, and perhaps most obviously, the close association of the *nakba* with Palestinian identity would make it exceptionally difficult for Palestinian politicians and negotiators to grapple with the most enduring consequence of the *nakba*—the refugee problem. The Palestinian refugees' experience of dispossession, exile, and disenfranchisement spurred the creation of and bolstered support for the Palestinian national movement years before Israel occupied the West Bank and Gaza Strip. The vindication of refugees' rights, moreover, would become particularly central to the approach of Fateh, the faction that eventually came to dominate Palestinian politics and, later, to negotiate with Israel: "The driving force in the philosophy and ideological outlook of Fateh, to the extent they existed, was profoundly existential. It derived overwhelmingly from the physical circumstances and deep alienation of the majority of uprooted and exiled refugees, rather than the minority of Palestinians who still resided in their homes after the 1948 war."[18] After committing to end this "bitter surrender" and the "terrifying reality that the children of the *nakba* experience everywhere" as the only means of restoring the "self confidence and capabilities" of the Palestinian people,[19] Fateh officials would find it difficult years later to discuss a compromise with respect to refugee return with Israel or even among themselves.

A fourth major consequence of the *nakba* was fragmentation of Palestinian political life. Although, as described above, the experience of dispossession and exile played a powerful role in consolidating Palestinian identity, its practical effect was to disperse the Palestinian population across the territory of many other states, rendering national political organization difficult and, at times, dangerous. The PLO would compensate for these circumstances in a variety of ways, from forming flexibly structured and loosely connected forums for promoting local political action to creating subnational governments in areas where Palestinians were concentrated (such as the disastrous "state within a state" in southern Lebanon). These efforts, however, would not succeed in preventing the creation of multiple Palestinian communities in the Middle East, each with its own array of interests, priorities, and allegiances.[20] Nor would they stem the burgeoning factionalism and external interference in Palestinian politics. As discussed further in the next section of this chapter, the legacy of disorganization and suspicion resulting from this fragmentation would continue to have a profound influence on Palestinian politics throughout the Oslo era, affecting Palestinian negotiating styles and positions.

The *nakba* would also influence the style of Palestinian negotiatiors in other ways. As described above, the experiences of dispossession and statelessness meant that, for many decades, Palestinians lacked control not only over their present and future circumstances but also over their past. They faced an adversary that rejected the notion of a "Palestinian" narrative, as expressed most notoriously in former Israeli prime minister Golda Meir's remark that "there was no such thing as Palestinians. . . . They did not exist."[21] Many in the Palestinian national movement believed that Arab governments also aimed to suppress Palestinian identity,[22] and some Arab governments provided ample evidence in support of that view.[23] Moreover, lacking a state, Palestinians also for the most part lacked control over their children's educational curricula and the attendant capacity to develop and propagate their own national narrative. This consistent lack of opportunity to tell the Palestinian story, and to feel that it had been heard, likely contributed to the tendency of Palestinian officials to dwell on history and principle in negotiations with Israel. It also fueled their desire for recognition of the legitimacy of the Palestinian narrative as they conceived it.

Finally, the fact that the defining moment in Palestinian history was a loss of cataclysmic proportions would make a sense of victimization one of the deepest strains in Palestinian identity. Uri Savir writes, "I came to understand that the Palestinians' perception of the balance of power was . . . a dwarf facing down a giant."[24] That perception left many Palestinians with the conviction that *sumud* (steadfastness)—expressed through patience and passive resistance and based on the hope that, left to its own devices, the enemy would defeat itself—was the best response to circum-stances that appeared to present few other options. Along with Palestinians' actual lack of political and military power, at least relative to Israel and the Arab states, this combined sense of victimization and steadfastness would lead Palestinians to engage in what one former Israeli negotiator de-scribes as "negotiations on the basis of weakness": passivity, particularly with respect to developing and presenting proposals; assertions of entitle-ment; and a desire for third-party involvement.[25]

Military Occupation

Israel's military occupation of the West Bank and Gaza Strip following the June 1967 war reinforced many of the aspects of Palestinian identity and experience spurred by the *nakba*. Under occupation, Palestinians in the West Bank, including East Jerusalem, and the Gaza Strip lacked con-trol over their economic activity, the allocation and management of their natural resources, and their ability to move. Barghouthi writes, "Occupa-tion prevents you from managing your affairs in your own way. It inter-feres in every aspect of life and of death; it interferes with longing and anger and desire and walking in the street. It interferes with going any-where and coming back, with going to market, the emergency hospital, the beach, the bedroom, or a distant capital."[26] Hundreds of thousands of Pales-tinians who, like Barghouthi, were displaced during the 1967 war were not allowed to return to their homes in the occupied territories, while hundreds more were deported for political activity. Moreover, Israel's settlement enterprise re-created the dynamic of losing land to Jewish settlers that had animated Palestinian peasant resistance to the Zionist movement after the second *aliya* (1904–14). Thus, the experience of occupation served to deepen the central features of the *nakba* experience—lack of control, dis-possession, disenfranchisement, and exile.

Israel's military occupation of the West Bank and Gaza Strip would also have a profound effect on Palestinian political organization. On the one hand, the crushing defeat of the Arab states in the 1967 war turned Palestinians away from the Arab states to the guerilla movements who were seen to be advocating a "Palestine first" approach.[27] On the other hand, the occupation shifted the center of Palestinian political life from inside Palestine to outside it. The failure of Fateh and other groups to consolidate a power base on Palestinian soil after 1967, combined with repression by Israeli military authorities, left political institutions within the occupied territories stunted. It also spawned an increasing disconnection between the leadership of the Palestinian national movement outside the occupied territories and the Palestinian population inside. The size and significance of these gaps would become apparent when the PLO returned to the West Bank and Gaza Strip within the framework of the Oslo Accords.

The Palestinian *intifada* ("shaking off") that broke out in December 1987 brought the worst aspects of Israeli occupation into sharper relief for Palestinians throughout the West Bank and Gaza Strip and served to bolster their sense of national identity. The brutality and scale of Israel's attempt to suppress the uprising (including then defense minister Yitzhak Rabin's declared policy of using "force, might, and beatings"),[28] coupled with the economic devastation it wrought,[29] meant that few Palestinian families were left untouched by the experience of military occupation. At the same time, the intifada launched a process of political re-empowerment among Palestinians in the occupied territories, as well as an effort to achieve greater economic self-reliance.[30] Indeed, during its first year at least, the intifada operated on the basis of a new model of Palestinian political organization, characterized by "voluntary, grass-roots activism, social mobilization, and decentralized leadership."[31] This model permitted much broader participation in Palestinian political life by West Bank and Gaza Strip residents, who were enabled "to influence the PLO's political positions more strongly and directly, to play a major role in determining the national political agenda, and to transform the accepted national tactics."[32] As discussed further below, this model would contrast starkly with the political system introduced by the PLO during the Oslo years, and resentment about that transformation would color many Palestinians' perceptions of their political leadership and its handling of negotiations.

Interim Self-Government

The experience of interim self-government within the framework of the Oslo Accords contributed to shaping the Palestinians' approach to negotiations in a variety of ways, deepening already-existing Palestinian political dynamics and creating new dynamics as the Palestinian national movement undertook for the first time to negotiate and implement agreements with Israel. As described below, a combination of internal legitimacy problems, diminishing confidence in the Israeli government's good faith, and poor circumstances on the ground placed extraordinary pressure on Palestinian negotiating teams.

Palestinians in the West Bank and Gaza Strip received the PLO's return to Palestine as a mixed blessing. Thousands lined the streets to celebrate their reunion with their long-exiled national leadership, and many more welcomed their first tastes of autonomy and self-government: Mourid Barghouthi, for example, writes of visiting the new Palestinian Ministry of Civil Affairs in Ramallah: "This is the location for the daily exhaustion and bitterness for thousands of Palestinians throughout the years that Ramallah was occupied. Their problems are still there, complex and difficult to solve, but now a smile meets them in the place that—since 1967 —witnessed constant attempts to humiliate them."[33] At the same time, after years of dispersal and fragmentation, the Oslo Accords permitted the beginnings of a process of "recentering"; Rashid Khalidi writes: "One unique circumstance is that although not sovereign or independent, and indeed bound by myriad restrictions imposed by the agreements with the Israelis, the new Palestinian Authority has more power over more of its people in more of Palestine than any Palestinian agency has had in the twentieth century."[34] These accomplishments, practical and psychological, fueled support for the Palestinian Authority and the peace process.

Over time, however, a variety of factors undermined confidence in the Palestinian leadership and the deal they had reached. As Hanan Ashrawi puts it, "The gods descend from Olympus, and suddenly we realize they're frail."[35] Local political activists and representatives of civil society organizations, both groups of which had played central roles in political organization during the first Palestinian intifada beginning in 1987, found themselves increasingly marginalized by the new regime. Returnees tended to monopolize positions of influence in government and undertook to eliminate factions and nongovernmental organizations that competed for political influence and foreign funds. Moreover, persistent and substantiated allegations of corruption and mismanagement, as well as torture, detention, intimidation, and censorship, served to erode the legitimacy of Palestinian government. By April 2000, three months before the summit at Camp David, 71 percent of Palestinians in the West Bank and Gaza Strip believed that corruption existed in Palestinian Authority institutions, 65 percent believed that people were unable to criticize the Palestinian Authority without fear, and only 22 percent evaluated Palestinian democracy positively.[36]

The most significant blow to the legitimacy of the Palestinian leadership, and source of pressure in subsequent negotiations, however, was the failure of the Oslo Accords to yield substantial improvements in the lives of Palestinians. As the Oslo agreements were implemented—or failed to be—Palestinians grew more acutely aware of the concessions to which their leadership had agreed. In particular, the rapid growth of Israeli settlements in the occupied territories elicited criticism of the PLO's failure to secure an explicit commitment to a settlement freeze, and the sporadic imposition of severe restrictions on Palestinian movement raised questions about the wisdom of the complex jurisdictional scheme established by the agreements and the overriding control reserved by Israel.

The Palestinian leadership attempted to compensate for these shortcomings in ways that would shape future negotiations. For example, they drew a firm distinction between the interim stage and permanent status. Even at times when negotiations regarding interim obligations and the permanent status were proceeding simultaneously, the Palestinian side insisted that they be kept separate and that interim obligations be scrupulously fulfilled. These demands frustrated the Israeli negotiating team, who felt that the interim issues would quickly be forgotten once a comprehensive settlement was reached.[37] In public, moreover, Palestinian leaders heated up their rhetoric regarding contentious permanent status issues such as refugees and borders. Ashrawi observes, "The PLO leadership had no sense of constituency. . . . When they came back and started seeing the consequences of having no legitimacy, . . . they decided they had to up the ante and have a public discourse that was so exaggerated to appeal to everybody."[38] The pressure not to betray the expectations created by this discourse would later constrain not only the flexibility of Palestinian positions in the talks but also the capacity of Palestinian officials to engage in internal discussions and preparations. In Ashrawi's words, they became "captives of their slogans."[39]

The experience of negotiating interim arrangements with Israel also influenced subsequent Palestinian negotiating behavior. In broad terms, Palestinian negotiators came to question whether they had bargained hard enough: Palestinian negotiator and minister Yasser Abed-Rabbo recalls, "I remember once Haim Ramon came to meet Arafat in Gaza . . . and he said something amazing which I still remember. He said, 'I met Uri Savir, and he told me that we made a very good agreement. Instead of being islands in a Palestinian sea for the settlements, Palestinians are islands in our sea now.' I was speechless. Those words stayed with me."[40]

Palestinian negotiators came to feel particularly burned by what they perceived as Israeli bad faith in interpreting the numerous ambiguous formulations in the agreements, which, inter alia, required the release of "prisoners" without stipulating how many,[41] provided for Israeli redeployment from West Bank "territory" without indicating how much,[42] and called for "free and normal" movement of Palestinian persons and goods "without derogating from Israel's security powers and responsibilities."[43] Similarly, Palestinians believed that they had received assurance that Israel would unilaterally freeze settlement activity even though it was not explicitly written into the agreement.[44] By the end of the 1990s, however, hundreds of Palestinian prisoners remained in Israeli jails, most West Bank territory remained under full Israeli control, Israeli checkpoints restricted Palestinian movement between cities and abroad, and settlement activity had doubled. As a result, Palestinians became extremely distrustful of unwritten promises and bilateral dispute resolution structures, which, they came to realize, left Israel total discretion in interpreting agreements.

Thus, the experience of interim self-government did little to address the key problems presented by the *nakba* and the experience of military occupation: the lack of control resulting from statelessness, the emphasis on territory prompted by dispossession, and the insecurity of exile. Indeed, for many Palestinians it served instead to deepen these experiences. Palestinians consequently came to regard permanent-status negotiations, which the Oslo architects conceived as the final stage of a relationship-building process, as a critical opportunity to change the terms of the relationship.

Political Organization

Palestinian political organization during the Oslo process was shaped both by the operating style of the PLO, and of Arafat in particular, and by Israel's continued control over the majority of the occupied territories. Although neither factor made the result of negotiations inevitable, both influenced the manner in which Palestinians negotiated.

A senior Fateh official once described PLO political organization as a "genius for failure."[45] Regrettably, after Oslo, the political power structure in the West Bank and Gaza Strip rapidly came to replicate preexisting

PLO dynamics. In Tunis, Arafat had "distributed funds freely to individuals in all spheres and areas and encouraged the emergence of a large and uncoordinated network of beneficiaries who reported directly to him,"[46] and he used the same tactics to consolidate his power base in the West Bank and Gaza Strip. As one Palestinian Authority minister reportedly complained in 1996, "Everything must be approved [by Arafat], from a request for a vacation by a Commerce Ministry employee, to whether one of his cars should have its muffler repaired, to whether X or Y should attend the next meeting with the Israelis. . . . That's the way he stays on top: everything has to pass through him."[47] Similarly, Arafat continued to pursue a policy of "creating numerous, parallel agencies and departments . . . as a means of fragmenting rival power bases and reinforcing his own control."[48] In this vein, he established multifarious security agencies, civil ministries, and departments with overlapping responsibilities and declined to resolve jurisdictional conflicts among ministries definitively, instead intervening personally and in an ad hoc manner to address individual disputes. The result was weak institutions and a competitive, internally divided leadership. As one Palestinian minister laments, "We have leaders; we don't have a leadership."[49]

These leaders, moreover, grew increasingly remote from both the Palestinian public and the rank and file of popular political movements that had represented an important power base. Arafat's reliance on the advice of a close circle of political advisers, who controlled access of both persons and information to the PLO chairman, "weakened the charismatic element of his leadership in a way that distribution of patronage from his office has not compensated."[50]

These problems were exacerbated by Israel's retention of overriding control over most aspects of Palestinian life during the interim period. Movement between areas under Palestinian jurisdiction required Israeli approval; access to resources such as water, electricity, and electromagnetic frequencies (necessary for mobile telecommunications) was coordinated through committees dominated by Israelis; and the incremental negotiation and implementation of interim arrangements placed many Palestinian officials in the role of supplicants to their Israeli counterparts. As a result, Palestinian politics grew increasingly multipolar, Palestinian officials recognizing that good relations with Israel could yield enhanced political (and economic) power in Palestinian structures. Combined with the deinstitutionalization of Palestinian politics by Arafat, these dynamics yielded not only chaos but also real and perceived conflicts of interest, which further eroded the Palestinian Authority's tenuous legitimacy.

As described further in the second and third sections of this chapter, these aspects of Palestinian political organization crippled Palestinian performance in negotiations. Centralized decision making decreased efficiency and stymied planning and coordination. Moreover, the competition among Palestinian institutions and officials for funding and political power encouraged information and resource hoarding, discouraged unorthodox thinking and open debate, and resulted in the communication of mixed messages about Palestinian capacities or positions. These problems by no means made a peace agreement impossible—had the Palestinians received a proposal from the Israeli team that came close to satisfying what they assessed to be their basic needs, it seems likely they would have embraced it and implemented it (though perhaps imperfectly)—but these problems did place additional pressure on a process that contained few mechanisms for constructively addressing the weaknesses of or misbehavior by the two sides.

Religious and Ethnic Affiliation

For most Palestinians, Palestine is unquestionably part of the larger Arab and Muslim worlds. The Palestinian national movement's relationship with Arab nationalism and political Islam, however, has been more ambivalent, Palestinians sometimes playing the role of standard-bearer for both, while at other times undertaking to carve out a niche independent of either. Palestinian negotiating behavior has reflected these tensions.

Islam

Religion has played an important role in Palestinian identity formation and politics since the beginning of the Palestinian national movement early in the twentieth century. Rashid Khalidi submits that "first among the factors [that caused the Arab population of Palestine to identify with the country in the years immediately before World War I] was a religious attachment to Palestine as a holy land on the part of Muslims and Christians (as well as by Jews, of course)."[51] After the *nakba*, moreover, political Islam, as propagated by the Muslim Brotherhood Society, was among the few organizing forces in Palestinian refugee camps[52] and shaped the approach of a number of leading figures in the Palestinian national movement, including Arafat.[53] Although the Islamists were eclipsed—and for a time suppressed—as a result of Gamal Abdel-Nasser's rise as a pan-Arab leader, their resurgence in the past two decades has been among the most important transformations in Palestinian politics. Baruch Kimmerling and Joel Migdal observe, "The growth of Islam as a political-religious force in Palestine has been largely a home-grown phenomenon. Rooted in local community aid and service institutions, [the Islamic movement] has developed a distinctive understanding of *jihad* in the context of Israeli rule. And, through that, [it] has made itself the largest and most important opposition force in the territories."[54] As the key competitor to the Palestinian Authority, the Islamist opposition has been able to exert influence on Palestinian politics both directly and indirectly, the Palestinian leadership undertaking to co-opt Islamist symbols and public figures.[55]

The personal and political importance of Islam to Palestinians affected their approaches to negotiations with Israel in several respects. The strength of the Islamists and the popular appeal of their political message, particularly among the segments of the Palestinian refugee community that had benefited least from the Oslo process, constrained the Palestinian leadership's capacity to promote compromise solutions. Moreover, it obliged them to cloak their positions in increasingly religious rhetoric. On the other hand, in negotiation sessions Palestinian officials tended to raise the specter of Muslim outrage—at home and abroad—as a means of justifying their positions on semireligious questions such as sovereignty over the Haram al-Sharif/Temple Mount.[56]

Even so, religion appears not to have been solely a tactical consideration. As a senior Palestinian negotiator recounts:

> On our side the cultural problem interfered with respect to the issue of al-Haram. For Arafat it was the main issue. He could have put this issue to the side, left it to the end. . . . But he was captivated by the fear that he is touching the holy. He was afraid of the myths of history, that he is touching something divine, that he should not compromise on it. . . . Arafat imprisoned himself in his own beliefs—the religious . . . beliefs of the 40s and 50s. "This belongs to Muslims; it should not be touched." This became the main thing. [His beliefs] became the directive which led him in the negotiating process. To a certain extent, I felt he became a mullah.[57]

Whether genuine or tactical, Arafat's religious objections to American-Israeli proposals regarding sovereignty over the Haram al-Sharif would be cited by some as the primary impediment to the successful outcome of the Camp David summit.[58]

Arab Nationalism

Since the beginning of the past century, Palestinians have struggled to reconcile their vision of Palestine as an integral part of a unified Arab nation with their lack of confidence in the Arab states' commitment to Palestinian independence. In the early 1920s, for example, after the betrayal by and fall of Emir Faysal's nationalist government in Damascus, Palestinian journalists turned from advocating a vision of Palestine as "Southern Syria," a vision steeped in Arab nationalist aspirations, to celebrating Palestine's and Palestinians' distinctive virtues.[59] Similarly, in the 1950s and 1960s, while many Palestinians turned to Nasser's vision of pan-Arab unity as the vehicle for liberating their homeland, key figures in the Fateh movement strategized about how "to extricate the Palestinian from the grasp of Arab patronage, party feuds, and Arab regional designs, and to return him to his natural place as a human being who has lost his land and must strive to recover it."[60]

These tensions remained evident in Palestinian rhetoric during the Oslo process. For example, in one of his articles describing the Camp David summit, Akram Hanieh begins by lamenting the weakness and fragmentation of the Arab world; then he evokes the banner of Arab nationalism, casting the Palestinians as the sole remaining soldiers for the cause: "[Arafat] realized the responsibility of entering a battle in the name of the Palestinian people, Arab nations, Muslims, and Christians. In these bad and difficult times, the Palestinian had to enter the battle of defending Jerusalem on behalf of all. He had to defend the Holy City that was linked to eternal names starting with the Islamic Caliph Omar Bin Al-Khattab, and ending with Salah Al-Deen Al-Ayyoubi; and he and his people entered the war on their own."[61]

As discussed further in the next section, Palestinian negotiators would attempt both to evoke and to dissociate themselves from the Arab and Islamic worlds as a means of exerting pressure on their Israeli counterparts. In turn, Arab leaders played a variety of roles in Palestinian-Israeli negotiations, from urging the Palestinians to show reasonableness in defining their negotiating positions (as Egyptian and Jordanian leaders did after President Clinton presented his "parameters"), to pressing the United

States and Israel to show sensitivity with respect to the disposition of delicate questions such as sovereignty over the Haram al-Sharif/Temple Mount (as Saudi and Egyptian leaders did after Camp David), to presenting an altogether different model for resolving the conflict (as Syria and Hizballah were perceived to have done following Israel's unilateral withdrawal from southern Lebanon, which many Palestinians saw as a vindication of the use of force). Palestinian officials sometimes requested these interventions and sometimes resented them, reflecting the ambivalence characteristic of Palestine's relationship with the larger Arab and Islamic worlds.

Palestinian Negotiating Patterns: A Portrait

How do Palestinians negotiate? As discussed in the previous section, the experience of the Palestinian people over the past century has been varied. That experience has tended to produce multiple strands of identity, a fragmented political culture, and, by extension, a variety of negotiating styles. Indeed, the 1990s witnessed two different Palestinian approaches to negotiations with Israel: the Washington talks that grew out of the Madrid Peace Conference in 1991, in which Palestinians from the West Bank and Gaza Strip participated as part of a joint Palestinian-Jordanian delegation; and the Oslo process (from 1993 through early 2001), in which representatives of the PLO and eventually the Palestinian Authoirty participated directly.

According to those involved, the two sets of talks involved different Palestinian negotiating styles. Ashrawi, who participated in the Washington talks, suggests that the Palestinians' approach in Washington "couldn't have been more different" from the approach during the Oslo process.[62] She contrasts what she sees as the Oslo negotiators' passivity, secretiveness, and lack of strategy with the efforts of the Washington delegation to take the initiative, engage the Palestinian public, and define clear goals. Saeb Ereikat, who participated in both sets of talks, acknowledges that there were differences of style but argues that the comparison is inapt: "I wouldn't call the Washington track negotiations. It was a learning process for us. We were a group who was set up to be used. The PLO wanted us to be the bridge for them to cross toward recognition with Israel and the U.S. Shamir wanted to use us against the PLO. The Americans wanted to test us for our ability to be leaders or not. I don't think anybody took us as negotiators."[63]

It is academic to speculate about how the Washington track would have ended had it not been supplanted by the Oslo process. In light of the Washington experience, however, it bears emphasizing that the patterns of Palestinian negotiating behavior that are the subject of this study neither reflect all Palestinians' negotiating styles nor are a necessary consequence of Palestinian history and experience. With that in mind, this section provides a portrait of Palestinian negotiating behavior during the Oslo process, examining the Palestinians' overall concept of negotiations, their approach to team composition and preparation, and their use of compromise, language, pressure and third-party involvement, law, and public opinion.

Overall Concept of Negotiations

The Palestinian team's overall concept of negotiations was shaped by three central factors. First, the Palestinian leadership sought to establish a firm distinction between interim accords and a permanent peace settlement. The Palestinians who negotiated the interim agreements offered concessions based on the understanding that they applied to short-term arrangements only and did not compromise Palestinian rights with respect to a permanent settlement. Even so, as described above, the practical consequences of these concessions sorely tested Palestinians' confidence in their leadership. Accordingly, the Palestinian leadership came to see a permanent-status agreement as an opportunity to correct earlier errors and, thereby, to vindicate the path they had chosen for their people.

Second, Palestinians entered the negotiations with the view that, in accepting UN Security Council Resolution 242 and the principle of land for peace, they had already made their historic compromise. Their efforts during the first six months of permanent-status talks were focused on convincing Israel and the United States of this premise, rather than on developing detailed proposals for implementing their vision for peace. Third, Palestinian negotiators came to the table with a sense of themselves, forged by their experience both before Oslo and during it, as the weaker party, saddled with circumstances not of their choosing and obliged to rely on others to level the playing field. As discussed below, these factors affected the way that Palestinians prepared for negotiations and the tactics they used during them.

Team Composition and Dynamics

Throughout the Oslo process, key Palestinian policy decisions—regarding both core political questions and issues of process (such as who would negotiate, when, and where)—were made by Chairman Arafat in consultation with a narrow circle of close advisers. During interim negotiations, decisions regarding negotiating team composition were sometimes based on a given person's expertise or experience; more often, however, Arafat selected negotiators based on more overtly political considerations, such as how a person would be received by Israeli counterparts, what constituency he or she represented, and whether he or she had shown appropriate loyalty in the recent past. Arafat's office, moreover, tended to micromanage negotiations, particularly those related to security or finance, at times reversing decisions made by senior negotiators—or replacing them late in the talks. This combination of politicking and micromanagement contributed to Palestinian negotiators' tendency to be both passive and competitive—unable to make decisions without consulting Arafat and concerned about who might replace them if they failed to achieve a deal. This behavior elicited complaints from both Palestinian negotiators[64] and Israeli negotiators.[65] Indeed, one Israeli negotiator observed that the lack of structure on the Palestinian side obliged Palestinian negotiators to use a "combination of panache and coercion" to unite the various personalities in their delegation.[66]

These problems became even more acute during permanent-status negotiations. The Palestinian "Leadership Committee"—comprising Palestinian Authority ministers and PLO officials selected by Arafat—was convened to discuss the negotiations periodically, but the frequency of their meetings diminished over the course of permanent-status talks. The committee, moreover, tended to be a forum better suited to political posturing than deliberative decision making: in the first months of the negotiations, it met to critique proposed speeches and to receive progress reports from negotiators—both sometimes provoking fiery arguments—but it did not seriously address the scale and nature of potential concessions, which would be discussed with members of the committee privately and informally, if at all.

Despite the narrowness of decision-making circles, Palestinian negotiating teams were often large, particularly at the beginning of the negotiations process. Several factors contributed to this. First, participation in the negotiations served as another form of patronage for Arafat—of showing favor (or disfavor) and of co-opting adversaries. The importance of the file assigned to a negotiator was one indicator of status in the Palestinian political structure. Second, coordination was limited, with little effort in advance of negotiation sessions to define an agenda or goals, making the sessions themselves the primary forum in which negotiators and support teams met to discuss positions. Third, the lack of clarity regarding what would be discussed, and potentially decided, at negotiations made it preferable to have "all hands on deck."

In addition, the roles of various participants were rarely defined with clarity: politicians sometimes engaged in legal drafting, Jerusalem experts found themselves in sessions about security, and legal advisers were called upon to prepare technical briefs. One PLO adviser recounts, "The composition of the team on the Israeli side was much more departmental. On our side it was much more ad hoc—more whimsical—based on the political."[67] In this regard, it is telling that of the twelve places allocated to the Palestinian team at Camp David, all but one were taken by politicians or political advisers to Arafat (in contrast to the Israeli team, which also included professional and administrative staff). Efforts to systematize the process of determining who would participate in negotiations—either internally or in tandem with the Israelis—met with little success. For example, rules set by the PLO Negotiations Affairs Department about the number and type of support staff who should attend negotiation sessions were often ignored or implemented incompletely. Similarly, although the parties negotiated a protocol on negotiations procedures, which required joint definition of agendas, advance sharing of participants' names, and so forth, the agreed-upon text was roundly ignored.

Perhaps the most salient characteristic of Palestinian negotiating teams, however, was the fierce competition among negotiators. With the apparent intention of letting a hundred flowers bloom, Chairman Arafat authorized multiple negotiation tracks, at times simultaneously; he continually altered the composition of negotiating teams; and he often gave unclear guidance regarding what he sought to achieve. The result was a high degree of mutual suspicion among negotiators, each of whom sought to be the man who brought home the deal but feared being disparaged as weak or traitorous by his competitors.

This predicament led some negotiators to prefer secret talks with Israelis.[68] Israeli negotiators, in turn, would subsequently complain that the Palestinians had expressed boldness in private but then retreated from (or even denied) earlier ideas once they were exposed in public. One PLO adviser describes the dynamic as follows, "You're not ready to make a compromise because you don't have the political backing of your leadership and you'll be screwed domestically. Your own domestic house was not in order; therefore any compromise that you make can be used against you. Of course, you did not have a partner that would reciprocate. But there was a culture of denigrating any achievement. Whatever you achieved was not good enough."

There were exceptions to this mode of operation. For example, negotiators in charge of the more technical and less political "state-to-state" issues such as economic relations tended to have more latitude for independent decision making; accordingly, they were often better positioned to define their mandate and goals in advance of negotiations and to take better advantage of technical and legal support. The rarity of these exceptions, however, proved the rule.

Preparation

The Palestinians prepared late for negotiations. During talks regarding interim arrangements, Israelis generally were the ones who tabled the first draft of a proposed agreement, including the Declaration of Principles,[69] the Gaza-Jericho agreement,[70] and the Ad Hoc Economic Agreement. This was in part because Palestinian negotiating teams tended not to define their fallback positions in advance, and they often operated without basic data regarding the issues they were negotiating. (Of course, some of this data was withheld by the Israeli side, which, for instance, prohibited Israeli suppliers from selling the Palestinians high-resolution aerial photographs of West Bank territory—even photographs in which military locations had been blacked out.) In 1996, Edward Said expressed concern that "a Palestinian negotiating style that has been neither well organized nor well stocked with both real experts and hard facts (including reliable maps, statistics, and minute knowledge of the changes instituted by Israel on the ground since 1948 and 1967) is simply going to repeat the mistakes . . . and passivity of the past."[71]

Said's concerns turned out to be well founded. Despite the establishment of committees to address each of the core permanent-status issues, little had been achieved by the resumption of permanent-status negotiations in November 1999 beyond articulating the core principles that formed the basis for the Palestinian consensus position. During the years that permanent-status negotiations were suspended by former Israeli prime minister Benjamin Netanyahu, the Palestinian leadership undertook to develop neither coherent proposals indicating how these principles could be implemented in practice nor fallback positions and compromise formulas. Instead, preparations initially focused on the development of arguments in support of the Palestinian position on relevant legal authorities, one Palestinian negotiator commissioning advisers to prepare three separate papers on the interpretation of UN Security Council Resolution 242. Actual policy work—mapping the contours of Palestinian positions in detail—did not commence in earnest until the spring of 2000, after negotiations were in full swing.

The focus of Palestinians' preparations arose in part from their negotiating strategy, which was to seek agreement on the key principles that would guide the talks before proceeding to discuss details. But that was not the only factor. On the eve of negotiations, it is unlikely that any of the negotiators seriously believed that the Palestinians would prevail on the Israeli team to accept the 1967 border without modifications or the return of four million refugees to their homes in what is now Israel. With public dissatisfaction with both the Palestinian Authority and the Oslo Accords on the rise, however, it would have been politically costly to authorize preparations of fallback positions. Facing this choice, Palestinian officials tended to send the decision up the political ladder and await further guidance. Alternatively, in some situations, competition among Palestinian departments for control over information brought preparations to a standstill: for example, the work of Palestinian legal advisers and refugee experts on refugee compensation issues came to a halt for months because a Palestinian diplomat who had received the relevant UN data refused to share it.

In addition to these political problems, the Palestinian leadership simply underestimated the amount of technical detail that would be involved in a peace agreement—in part because they believed that the parties' agreement to begin with a "framework agreement" meant that most details would be deferred to a final, "comprehensive" agreement. (As it turned out, because the parties were incapable of agreeing to broad principles, they were obliged to turn relatively quickly to details.) As a result, negotiators at times were able to respond only tentatively to Israeli proposals regarding technical subjects, perhaps deepening perceptions that they were not serious about reaching a peace deal. Regrettably, Palestinian support teams would feel fully prepared only by the start of the Taba talks—the last round before negotiations were suspended by Israeli prime minister Ariel Sharon.

Compromise

Unlike the Israeli teams, which from the beginning of the Oslo process arrived at negotiations with their red lines clearly defined,[72] Palestinians came to the table without clearly articulated goals—or a clear sense of their best alternative to a negotiated agreement if they failed to achieve those goals. Accordingly, during interim negotiations, Palestinians tended to agree to concessions at the eleventh hour, often without planning or calculation, and sometimes after browbeating by their Israeli counterparts.[73] Palestinian negotiators justified their concessions as necessary first steps toward establishing a foothold in Palestinian territory, emphasizing that these compromises related only to the interim period, not to permanent status.

Accordingly, during the early rounds of permanent-status negotiations, Palestinians tabled few concrete proposals for compromise, dwelling instead on the principles on which, they argued, solutions should be based. To a certain extent, this passivity arose from the conviction that the Israeli team, which tended to dictate its red lines without explaining them, was not putting all of its cards on the table and sought to "close the Palestinian deal at the lowest price."[74] Burned by the popular perception that they had given away too much too early during interim negotiations, the Palestinian leadership were reluctant to reveal their own hand for fear that proposed compromises would be regarded as a new starting point for negotiations. This fear was perhaps justified: after the Palestinian team expressed willingness during talks in Washington in December 2000 to consider Israel's annexation of up to 2 percent of the West Bank, then U.S. secretary of state Madeleine Albright told them, "You say you need 98 percent of the West Bank. The Israelis say they need it to be 92 percent. The obvious compromise is 94 to 96 percent." Gaza preventive security chief Mohammad Dahlan's pleas with the secretary to not reduce issues to bazaar-style bargaining fell on deaf ears.

As noted above, this approach also arose from the conviction that the Palestinians had already made their compromises. "For all the talk about peace and reconciliation," Hussein Agha and Robert Malley observe, "most Palestinians were more resigned to the two-state solution than they were willing to embrace it. . . . The war for the whole of Palestine was over because it had been lost. Oslo, as they saw it, was not about negotiating peace terms but terms of surrender. Bearing this perspective in mind explains the Palestinians' view that Oslo itself is the historic compromise—an agreement to concede 78 percent of mandatory Palestine to Israel."[75] In light of that compromise, Palestinians did not see it as their role to propose further compromises over the remaining 22 percent: if Israel sought further concessions, then it should make a case for why they were needed—and be prepared to compensate Palestinians for them.

Over the course of negotiations, however, Palestinian negotiators grew more proactive, probably for two primary reasons. First, as discussed above, their level of preparation increased significantly between the Camp David summit and the Taba talks, particularly with respect to technical questions that were central to the disposition of issues such as security and territory. Confronted with detailed Israeli proposals for the first time in the summer of 2000, Palestinians took time to formulate their responses and to consider where their own red lines actually stood. Second, the consensus among Palestinian politicians regarding those red lines shifted after Camp David, when a number of taboos were broken; negotiators consequently could feel more comfortable discussing issues such as Israel's annexation of certain settlements in East Jerusalem and other areas of the West Bank or the establishment of Israeli early-warning stations in the West Bank. This shift reduced the cost to negotiators and their support teams of exploring compromise solutions. (Nevertheless, even as late as the Taba talks, Palestinians referred to the maps they tabled merely as "illustrations," not proposals.)

Language

During interim-period negotiations, the way a proposed provision was phrased sometimes turned out to be as much a point of contention as what it provided for substantively. Former Israeli negotiator Uri Savir describes how the parties overcame an impasse near the conclusion of negotiations in Taba in 1995 over whether Palestinian police officers would be required to seek Israeli "approval" before traveling from area A to area B:

> "I didn't understand it that way," [Arafat] said, his voice hoarse. "You really want to humiliate me. Well, I prefer that there be no agreement."

... "Mr. Chairman," I said, "knowing my mandate for a compromise, I'm sure we can find a less offensive way of saying it in the text, and after three months we may change it to notification."

Arafat agreed, and I thanked him. Yoel [Singer] replaced the word "approval" with "confirmation."[76]

Palestinian negotiators remained sensitive about language choices in permanent-status negotiations. For example, in security talks in September 2000, Dahlan told his Israeli counterparts, "I understand that you don't want a militarized state that can attack Israel or assist others in attacking Israel. But we cannot accept the phrase 'demilitarized state.' I suggest 'a state with limited arms' or 'defensive arms.' Without using the phrase, we can reach an acceptable agreement. I don't want anything that sounds like the interim—the counting of bullets, etc."[77] Had negotiations continued, it is likely that some concerns could have been overcome by creative drafting.

At times, however, Israeli negotiators mistook their counterparts' substantive objections for sensitivities about word choices, as in the following exchange at the Taba talks about whether Israel would retain overriding control of Palestinian airspace:

> SHLOMO YANAI: I think you understand that there is no way to run day-to-day life without a solution in this case. And I think you understand that Israel must have overriding security [control].
> MOHAMMAD DAHLAN: I understand, but don't agree. We have experienced your "overriding" during the interim period and won't do it again. I cannot sanction experts on the basis of this principle. I'm offering you something better than what you have with the United States or Jordan. I understand that there are emergencies. I'm open to have coordination with you. . . . If the overriding is yours, then I have nothing. I'm not going to leave anything to good faith. I'll get you a list of the number of times planes coordinated with you were rejected for various reasons by your land control. For the permanent status, we have our airspace, our own traffic control, and on that basis we're prepared to discuss how to deal with emergencies and other special situations with you. But we say no to overriding Israeli control.
> YANAI: We can choose another word![78]

This exchange is important, not just as an example of misunderstood messages, but also for what it reveals about the differences between the parties' approaches to permanent status: Palestinians sought a clean break with the interim period both at the negotiating table and on the ground; Israelis, however, appeared neither to see permanent status as a fundamental transformation nor to appreciate that the Palestinians did.

Pressure and Third-Party Involvement

During interim negotiations, withholding an accomplishment was one of the few means available to Palestinians for pressuring Israeli counterparts. Arafat repeatedly engaged in brinkmanship, flying into a rage near the conclusion of a negotiation round and threatening to abandon the talks on the grounds that he could not face his people if he made concessions on key issues.[79] These tantrums, however, yielded little more than minor concessions from the Israelis.[80] (And Israeli officials sometimes used the same tactic.)[81] Accordingly, Palestinian negotiators entered permanent-status talks with the awareness, hard earned during the interim period, that bilateralism afforded the weaker party few levers for exerting pressure.

As a result, they sought to evoke—if not, always, to elicit—pressure from third parties: the United States, the Arab and Muslim worlds, and even the Palestinian domestic opposition. At Camp David, for example, Chairman Arafat defended the Palestinian rejection of Israeli sovereignty over the Haram al-Sharif by evoking Palestinian, Arab, and Muslim sentiment: "I can't betray my people. Do you want to come to my funeral? I'd rather die than agree to Israeli sovereignty over the Haram al-Sharif. . . . I won't go down in Arab history as a traitor."[82] Similarly, in security negotiations in September 2000, Saeb Ereikat raised the specter of inter-Arab conflict in arguing against Israeli emergency deployment in Palestinian territory:

> I'm an Arab. I'm not going to change—my son's name is Mohammad, and his son's name will be Saeb. Strategically speaking, if the concern is that Israel will be threatened from the East, which is the basis for all of these zones and arrangements, I'm faced with a dilemma. I cannot stop being an Arab in time of war, but I cannot be allies with those Arabs who would attack Israel. . . . I cannot let you use our territory against others. We will have to tell the Arab League and Islamic Conference what we've agreed. I don't want the Syrians to tell me that we've entered an alliance with Israel.[83]

Ereikat resumed this line several months later during security talks at Taba:

> [W]e are an Arab nation, Muslim and Christian, that wants to live in peace. I can tell you that we cannot, politically speaking, deny Arabs access of troops on our land, while agreeing [with] Israel to do this. It will disqualify us from the Arab league, and Islamic nation. . . . I am a small neutral nation. Clinton suggested we have international forces for the purpose of . . . deterrence. By deterrence, he clearly meant Israel's protection. His proposal will allow for the birth of a new international security system.[84]

In these interventions, one sees an attempt by the Palestinians to strike a delicate balance: on the one hand, they sought to increase their perceived strength (and the validity of their positions) by identifying themselves as part of larger, and stronger, communities (e.g., the Arab and Muslim worlds); on the other, they sought to dissociate themselves from any threat posed by these other parties, portraying themselves as small, neutral, and committed to Israel's protection.

Ultimately, however, Palestinians recognized that the only third party that could actually wield an influence over the negotiations process was the United States. When they succeeded in securing U.S. involvement, however, they would not always know what to do with it. Robert Malley recalls that, whereas the Israeli team was in constant contact with the U.S. peace team, making frequent substantive and procedural suggestions, Palestinian officials tended to be much more reticent.[85] Moreover, the special relationship between Israel and the United States left Palestinians with the impression—apparently not very far removed from reality—that Israeli and U.S. officials were colluding to pressure the Palestinians into a deal. Accordingly, Arafat and his delegation entered Camp David talks believing that the summit had been conceived as a trap.[86]

Law

In public advocacy, Palestinians make frequent references to "the international legality"—the array of UN resolutions and other legal instruments that support their claims. As one former PLO legal adviser observed, Palestinians—particularly those from inside the occupied territories—"were raised, in a sense, identifying the Palestinian cause with law."[87] In negotiations with Israel, however, Palestinian officials' attitudes toward both law and lawyers were more ambivalent. During interim-period negotiations, lawyers were generally consulted late: for example, despite the active involvement of an experienced Israeli legal adviser in drafting the Declaration of Principles, the Palestinians showed the draft to their own legal counsel (an Egyptian official) for the first time only a few weeks before the conclusion of the talks. Moreover, Palestinian negotiators apparently acquiesced to the Israeli view of international law as another point of contention rather than a framework for resolving disputes; as a consequence, discussion of international law appears to have been avoided as self-consciously as discussion of history.[88]

Stung by criticism about their failure to consult legal counsel when negotiating the Oslo Accords, Palestinian negotiators made more regular use of legal advisers in permanent-status negotiations. Moreover, in the early rounds of those talks, they made frequent allusions to international legal principles and sought to engage their Israeli counterparts in discussion about the legal framework for negotiations. In view of the deficit of rule of law in internal Palestinian governance, it may be that Palestinian negotiators' use of legal arguments was born of tactical motivations rather than a wholesale commitment to international law, but they did evoke law often at the negotiating table.

Legal arguments, however, were not well received by Israeli and U.S. officials. At one of the first negotiation sessions on borders issues, in December 1999, Israeli negotiators made clear that, from their perspective, law would not be a productive avenue of discussion. They argued that international law is useful only if both sides agree it is applicable and agree on its interpretation and that neither was the case in Palestinian-Israeli negotiations. President Clinton would show even greater impatience with legal arguments: near the beginning of the Camp David talks, when asked to comment on a map presented by the Israelis, Palestinian legislator Ahmed Qurei refused, stating, "The Israelis must first accept the principle of the exchange of territories. Besides, for the Palestinians, international legitimacy means Israeli retreat to the border of June 4, 1967." Clinton's response reportedly was explosive: "Sir, I know you'd like the whole map to be yellow [representing Palestinian territory]. But that's not possible. This isn't the Security Council here. This isn't the UN General Assembly. If you want to give a lecture, go over there and don't make me waste my time. . . . You're obstructing the negotiation. You're not acting in good faith."[89] These responses, repeated again and again by Israeli and U.S. officials, discouraged further legal interventions by the Palestinians.

By the end of negotiations, Palestinians tended to use legal arguments as a means of defining a general standard of reasonableness, rather than as a constraint on what could be agreed upon. For example, in interpreting Clinton's "ideas" regarding a territorial settlement, which called for the parties to develop a map consistent with, among other things, the criterion of "contiguity," Palestinians argued that Palestinian contiguity should trump Israeli contiguity in the West Bank since Israeli settlements were a violation of international humanitarian law in the first place. However, even within this framework, Palestinians and Israelis did not tend to engage in *legal* discussions of the issues; law was simply an element of the Palestinian attempt at persuasion. One notable exception was a meeting during the Taba talks between the legal advisers of both sides to address the parties' respective claims to the no-man's-land in the Latrun area; this session, however, appears to have been convened by the Israeli side primarily as a means of keeping the legal advisors from meddling in other negotiation sessions.

Public Opinion

Palestinian negotiators, like their Israeli counterparts, cited public opinion as a means of defining their limits for compromise and placing pressure on the other side. Chairman Arafat and other Palestinian leaders made particularly frequent reference to Palestinian public opinion early in the Oslo process, before elections were held. For example, Arafat told Shimon Peres that his capacity for compromise was constrained by the fact that he ruled "not on the basis of majority, but by virtue of [his] personal credit."[90] According to one Israeli negotiator, this argument succeeded in keeping at bay Israel's demands for explicit changes to the PLO charter and more decisive action against Islamists in the run-up to Palestinian elections in 1996.[91]

During permanent-status talks, however, these tactics yielded less success. For instance, during the Taba round, Saeb Ereikat argued against continued deployment of Israeli troops in the Jordan Valley by noting that "already the idea of international forces is causing us internal problems; Palestinians are saying this will be a banana republic."[92] This kind of argument, however, failed to convince Israeli negotiators, who expressed frustration with what they regarded as the Palestinian leadership's failure to lead their public. During one session at Camp David, Israeli foreign minister Shlomo Ben Ami screamed at a Palestinian legal adviser, "Your leaders don't deserve to have a state! They don't know how to seize an opportunity! They're obsessed by public opinion! They're not equal to this historical moment!"[93]

Palestinians leveled the same charges at Israeli negotiators.[94] It seems, however, that Palestinian officials regarded—and used—public opinion differently than their Israeli counterparts. A political adviser to the PLO explains the difference:

> The two sides have a different sense of public opinion. For Israelis, it's connected to elections, votes of confidence, etc. It's much more structured. Ours is very impressionistic. Of course, when we're negotiating we mention public opinion. But we never came with a poll. We would come and say public opinion will screw us, but we never produced the tools. We tend to think more about other power centers, instead. [The issue of] prisoners, for example, is not about the public; it's about trying to co-opt the factions.[95]

In retrospect, the loose structure of Palestinian political organization—and the lack of a robust democratic process—likely not only led Palestinian negotiators to invoke Palestinian public opinion in more impressionistic terms but also prompted Israeli and American officials to see such pleas as tactical and assign them little weight.

The negotiating patterns described above are hardly surprising in view of the Palestinians' historical experience and political organization. The political chaos that prompted fierce competition among Palestinian negotiators is difficult to distinguish from the PLO's modus operandi in the years preceding the Oslo Accords. The centralization of decision-making authority that facilitated the secret channels that gave rise to the Oslo process also served to stymie effective preparation for and public participation in subsequent negotiations. And the flexibility of Palestinian officials in negotiating interim-period agreements effectively curtailed their latitude for compromise with respect to a permanent settlement by undermining their popular legitimacy. In sum, none of the patterns described above is easily disentangled from the others.

It also bears noting that many Palestinian negotiators were well aware of the frailties in the negotiation culture of which they were part. In private settings and individual conversations, they were quick to criticize the general approach being taken and often even anticipated mistakes that would be made as a result of structural and personality factors in Palestinian political life. None of them, however, seems to have felt able to effect a change or even to create the political space within which criticism might be channeled to some constructive end. That inability appears to have stemmed in part from Palestinian political organization and in part from the attitudes of Israeli counterparts, which, as discussed below, also shaped Palestinian negotiating behavior.

Cultures Crossed: Palestinian-Israeli Negotiating Dynamics

Participants from all sides of the peace talks balk at the notion that differences in style or culture determined the result of the negotiations. Aaron Miller observes, "I never cease to be amazed by how many people try to project onto Arafat this image of the wandering Bedouin sheikh, leading his people from oasis to oasis, culturally wired against committing to a permanent arrangement. . . . Of the many explanations I've heard for the failure to make peace in the Middle East, this seems the least persuasive —and, potentially, very dangerous."[96] One Palestinian political adviser was similarly skeptical about the influence of culture, particularly once negotiations began in earnest: "At Camp David, the culture was there— the infighting, lack of clear mandates—but it was insignificant compared to the politics of things; it was badly managed in many ways."[97] A former Israeli negotiator goes a step further, arguing that the negotiation styles of the two sides were more alike than different: "What cultural differences? The Israelis and the Palestinians are much closer to one another as nations in terms of mentality, attitude, everything, including ways of negotiations, internal collaboration—you name it—than each one of them is versus the Norwegians, the Americans, even the Egyptians."[98]

Certainly, the failure of permanent-status negotiations to yield a historic peace settlement was the result of a variety of factors, including significant substantive disagreements. In the following respects, however, the way Palestinians and Israelis negotiated with each other likely contributed to "incorrect attribution of motive[s]"[99] and, ultimately, to their inability to reach agreement.

Israeli negotiators' unwillingness to discuss the history of the conflict led their Palestinian counterparts to the conclusion that they had not come to terms with it—or with them. As discussed in the preceding section, for Palestinians the peace process represented an opportunity not only to establish control over their own lives in their own independent state but also to obtain recognition—and validation—of the legitimacy of their national narrative. From the start of permanent-status negotiations, however, Israelis expressed impatience with discussions about the past, arguing that they were a waste of time and would only deepen enmity between the parties.

Israeli attorney general Elyakim Rubinstein crystallized this view in comments during a session about refugees at Camp David: "Our vision is a humanitarian one. On the historical level, we can't agree to be held responsible for the refugee problem. What happened in 1948 is the subject of controversy, *and the peace process shouldn't be the arena in which historical truth is pronounced.*"[100]

For Palestinians, the Israelis' approach to history reflected an unwillingness to grapple with their nation's past, and the debt owed to its primary victims. Describing the session at which Rubinstein made the above comment, Palestinian journalist and political adviser Akram Hanieh writes:

> In the absence of seriousness on the part of Israel, the discussion revolved mostly around the past, not the present or the future. The clash and difference between the two visions goes back to the 1948 Palestinian *Nakba*, or catastrophe, to its very roots.
>
> [The Refugee Committee] was the most difficult committee because it was the reality committee, ruled by history. . . . It placed Israel in front of her direct victims, in front of the witnesses to its crimes.
>
> It was strange because Israeli *[sic]* continued to deny its crime. There is a complete denial of the *Nakba* and of the Israeli responsibility in causing it. . . . When the Israelis were presented with the memoirs and the testimonies of their own generals, they rejected them.[101]

This bitterness was compounded by the tendency of Israeli officials to speak in ways that suggested they did not recognize the historic compromise Palestinians already had made. As Hussein Agha and Robert Malley point out, "The notion that Israel was 'offering' land, being 'generous,' or 'making concessions' seemed to [Palestinians] doubly wrong—in a single stroke both affirming Israel's right and denying the Palestinians'. For the Palestinians, land was not given but given back."[102]

In retrospect, it is perhaps unlikely that discussions of historical narrative would have altered the two sides' positions in fundamental ways, particularly on issues as contentious as refugees and Jerusalem, and it is unknowable how they would have affected atmospherics in the negotiations. It is worthy of note, however, that at the Taba talks Israeli and Palestinian negotiators did, finally, discuss the history of the refugee problem and undertook to construct a joint narrative about it. Although the Israeli team did not substantially alter its position regarding Palestinian refugees' right of return, participants from the Palestinian side emerged feeling that the sessions had been productive. Describing the Israeli minister who led the refugee talks at Taba, one Palestinian adviser was heard to remark,

"That Yossi Beilin—his positions, in the end, might as well be Rubin-stein's. But the way he talks and listens—you can't help but trust him."

The tendency of Israeli negotiators to dictate positions without justifying them reinforced Palestinians' concern that Israelis were less interested in a new relationship of equality than in a modification of existing arrange-ments. Negotiations rarely involved frank discussion about the interests underlying either side's positions. Palestinians grew particularly frustrated with Israelis' refusal to explain "needs" that appeared to be arbitrarily de-fined. For example, Israeli negotiators consistently demanded the place-ment of three Israeli early-warning stations in the West Bank; when Palestinians argued that no more than two were required and pointed out that one of the proposed sites could easily be relocated to Israeli territory less than ten kilometers away, Israelis responded that only Israel could de-fine its security needs. Similarly, Israeli negotiators claimed at Taba that Israel "needs" to annex 80 percent of the settlers; the assertion elicited an explosive response from one of the Palestinian negotiators, who screamed, "Then I *need* 80% of the refugees to return. Or give me 50%, or 30%—even 10%!"[103]

Israeli officials, moreover, sometimes presented their positions as dic-tates, rather than proposals. For Palestinians, a nation seeking to control their own lives and land, this approach resonated in all of the wrong ways. The following exchange in security talks between Israeli negotiator Gilead Sher and Mohammad Dahlan reflects the tension:

> SHER: There are some elements—I told you from the first moment—that are not negotiable, but these are few.
> DAHLAN: There is nothing that is not negotiable. How many more years do you want to dominate us?[104]

The cumulative effect of this behavior was a Palestinian perception that Israel sought to impose a settlement on them: at Camp David, Chair-man Arafat remarked bitterly to President Clinton, "I have the impression that we're expected to keep quiet and wait for Mr. Barak to decide what's good for him and for us."[105] When Palestinians sought to involve or evoke third parties in the negotiations as a means of leveling the playing field, the Israelis' resistance to what they called a Palestinian attempt to "internationalize" the conflict only confirmed the Palestinian perception that Israel sought to exploit the power disparity between the parties and coerce a deal. Prime Minister Barak's sidelining of the Palestinians in favor of the Syrian track earlier in 2000 and his refusal to implement the "third further redeployment" of troops in the West Bank to which he had earlier committed (and for which he had received Knesset approval) also left Palestinians with the impression that they were being bamboozled.

Palestinian political disorganization resulted in the communication of mixed messages, which raised doubts about the Palestinians' commitment to—and capacity to implement—a peace agreement. Competition among Palestinian negotiators was a source of confusion and bitterness on all sides. In a letter to the *New York Review of Books,* Gidi Grinstein, the secretary to the Israeli negotiating team, complains, "On the Palestinian side, a fragmented leadership was consumed by brutal internal struggle over succession and political and economic power. . . . Rarely was there an integrated Palestinian position. Sometimes more than one Palestinian claimed to have the authority to negotiate. At other times, senior Palestinians would undermine their own official delegation. Anyone who sought to advance the negotiations was soon delegitimized. It was a messy collective paralysis."[106]

This competition stymied opportunities for the parties to assess the contours of potential compromises. For example, secret talks held by Ahmed Qurei and Hassan Asfour in Stockholm in May 2000 were brought to an early end by Palestinian officials involved in the formal rounds, who were incensed about being blindsided. This, in turn, led the Israelis to press prematurely for a summit at Camp David at which Arafat and all of his close advisers would be present. Palestinian political disorganization also led to the communication of mixed messages. Dennis Ross would criticize Arafat's failure at Camp David "to control the fratricidal competition in his delegation—effectively giving license to those who were attacking other members who were trying to find ways to bridge the differences."[107] Palestinians, moreover, felt that the competition among negotiators allowed Israel and the United States to exploit differences among them: "[T]here were certain elements in Palestinian politics and Arab politics," Ereikat observes, "that went to the Americans and led them to believe that if you present certain ideas, the Palestinians will accept. And the Americans without even bothering to ask those of us who are relevant chose to believe that—especially that Arafat would be satisfied with an office in the Old City—and the Americans locked on this and believed it would be doable. And those of us who said it would not fly became extremists."[108]

Palestinian negotiators' passivity reinforced the impression that they were not interested in actually reaching a deal. Palestinian negotiators failed not only to respond to Israeli and American ideas with compromise formulations of their own (at least not until late in the negotiations) but also to put forward convincing explanations of how the principles they advocated could be implemented. According to Agha and Malley, this passivity was the Palestinians' "principal failing" and contributed to an image of intransigence.[109] Yezid Sayigh shares that assessment, observing that it also undermined Israelis' inclination to make peace: "The most serious leadership failing has arguably been the absence of any sustained effort to deliver a specific political message to the Israeli government, parliamentary parties and voting public. Without clear enunciation of concrete Palestinian demands, Israeli audiences have been unable to calculate the comparative costs and benefits of pursuing one course of action or another toward the Palestinians (in contrast to the experience with Hizbollah). Their fallback has been to assume the worst about Palestinian intentions."[110] In the same vein (though perhaps self-servingly), Ehud Barak cites Arafat's failure to tender counterproposals as evidence of a lack of "the character or will" to make a historic compromise and of an intention to achieve Israel's demise through diplomatic means.[111]

Notably, when Palestinians did arrive at the negotiating table with fully developed proposals and coherent arguments in support of them, they achieved positive results. For example, in negotiations regarding Israeli-Palestinian economic relations at Emmitsburg (concurrent with the Camp David summit), the Palestinian negotiating team presented a draft framework agreement and explained in detail the needs underlying it, giving specific examples of how the Israeli team's proposals (which involved the maintenance of the status quo in some respects) had proved problematic during the interim period. When the United States presented a bridging proposal near the conclusion of the talks, it drew heavily (arguably primarily) from the Palestinian draft. Of course, the issues at stake were not as emotionally charged as the questions of Jerusalem or the refugees; however, the Palestinians' relative success at the economic talks (at least at convincing American moderators) provides some indication of what may be achieved through a more proactive approach.

Conclusion

The Oslo process presented Palestinian negotiators with a formidable array of challenges that were not of their own creation: an adversary with far greater political, military, and economic power, as well as the ear of the dominant power in a unipolar world; a people with extremely high hopes for, if not expectations in, the peace process as a vehicle for national vindication, as well as independence; and a constellation of regional allies who were as judgmental as they were unreliable. In light of these factors, it is unsurprising that the Palestinian leadership came to regard permanent-status negotiations as an opportunity to be survived rather than seized, and came consequently to see the failure of the talks at Camp David (and subsequently) as a kind of success.

This narrative, of course, is not new in Palestinian history. Rashid Khalidi writes, "In the Palestinian case, repeated, crushing failure has been surmounted and survived, and in some sense has been incorporated into the narrative of identity as triumph. . . . While drawing on undeniable verities . . . there can be little question that such a version of history conveniently absolves the Palestinians from the responsibility for their own fate. From this perspective, if their enemies were so numerous and powerful, it is hardly surprising that they were defeated."[112] In the present case, as well, there is no certainty that sounder leadership or more clever negotiating tactics would have enabled the Palestinians to overcome the odds stacked against them. As Palestinians undertake to identify the lessons to be learned from the Oslo experience, however, they will need to look unflinchingly at the ways in which their internal organization and strategies shaped the predicament in which they found themselves, and to complement their narrative of survival with an ethic of responsibility.

Israelis, too, must endeavor to understand the ways that their own negotiating behavior played a part in effecting problematic patterns in Palestinian governance and diplomacy. Palestinians' capacity to assume responsibility in a peace partnership will turn in great measure on Israelis' willingness to cede authority. The Oslo process makes clear that Palestinians will not behave as equal partners if the attitudes of their Israeli counterparts or the terms of their proposals place Palestinians in a position of subordination. Moreover, willful inattention to—or outright denial of—the historical experiences that animate Palestinian claims and demands will not make Palestinians any more apt to forget them. Indeed, in peacemaking, as in conflict, both sides would do well to remember that one of the many things that Palestinians and Israelis have in common is the narrative of survival in the face of great adversity.

Notes

This chapter is dedicated to the memory of my uncle, Ahmad Sidqi al-Dajani (1937–2003).

1. Arafat held the position not only of chairman of the PLO Executive Committee but also of president *(ra'ees)* of the Palestinian Authority. Because Arafat's involvement in negotiations sprang from his role as head of the PLO, which possesses the legal authority to represent the Palestinian people in international forums, he is referred to in this chapter as Chairman Arafat.

2. See Hussein Agha and Robert Malley, "Camp David: The Tragedy of Errors," *New York Review of Books,* August 9, 2001; Charles Enderlin, *Shattered Dreams: The Failure of the Peace Process in the Middle East, 1995–2002,* trans. Susan Fairfield (New York: Other Press, 2003); Deborah Sontag, "Quest for Middle East Peace: How and Why It Failed," *New York Times,* July 26, 2001; Clayton E. Swisher, *The Truth about Camp David: The Untold Story about the Collapse of the Middle East Peace Process* (New York: Nation Books, 2004).

3. Agha and Malley, "Camp David: An Exchange," *New York Review of Books,* September 20, 2001.

4. Gilead Sher, "Negotiating in Times of Crisis" (lecture, Wharton School, Philadelphia, August 18, 2003).

5. Saeb Ereikat, in discussion with the author, Jericho, August 14, 2003.

6. Raymond Cohen, *Negotiating across Cultures* (Washington, DC: United States Institute of Peace Press, 2002), 27.

7. Edward Said, *After the Last Sky* (New York: Pantheon Press, 1985), 38.

8. Rashid Khalidi, *Palestinian Identity: The Construction of Modern National Consciousness* (New York: Columbia University Press, 1997), 146.

9. Baruch Kimmerling and Joel S. Migdal, *The Palestinian People: A History* (Cambridge, MA: Harvard University Press, 2003), 135 (emphasis added).

10. Khalidi, *Palestinian Identity,* 22.

11. Ibid., 193.

12. Ibid., 153.

13. Yezid Sayigh, *Armed Struggle and the Search for State: The Palestinian National Movement, 1949–1993* (Oxford: Oxford University Press, 1997), 46.

14. Khalidi, *Palestinian Identity,* 1.

15. Mourid Barghouthi, *I Saw Ramallah,* trans. Ahdaf Soueif (New York: Anchor Books, 2003), 6.

16. Khalidi, *Palestinian Identity,* 114.

17. Sayigh, *Armed Struggle and the Search for State,* 46–47.

18. Ibid., 88.

19. Ibid., 88 (quoting interview with unidentified leader).

20. Kimmerling and Migdal, *The Palestinian People,* 402–403.

21. *Sunday Times* (London), June 15, 1969.

22. Sayigh, *Armed Struggle and the Search for State,* 89.

23. For example, on March 1, 1950, Jordan's King Abdullah banned use of the term "Palestine" in any official document or correspondence. Ibid., 42.

24. Uri Savir, *The Process: 1,100 Days That Changed the Middle East* (New York: Random House, 1998), 14.

25. Joel Singer, in discussion with the author, Washington, DC, September 2, 2003.

26. Barghouthi, *I Saw Ramallah,* 48.

27. Sayigh, *Armed Struggle and the Search for State,* 87–92.

28. Yezid Sayigh summarizes: "[A] host of punitive measures were imposed on the civilian population. One was the closure of 900 schools, while curfews prevented tens of thousands of Palestinian labourers from commuting to work in Israel. . . . Over 2,600 Palestinians were in administrative detention by September according to a U.S. State Department report, and a total of 40,000 were arrested in the first eighteen months of the uprising, a handful of whom were expelled to South Lebanon." Sayigh, *Armed Struggle and the Search for State,* 619 (citing Israeli and American sources).

29. Kimmerling and Migdal describe the magnitude of the problem as follows: "In the first three years of the Intifada, Palestinians in Gaza saw a 30 percent decline in their gross national product; a drop in per capita income from $1,700 to $1,200, with some families losing as much as three-quarters of their income; a 75 percent decline in remittances from outside; and a sharp drop in income from work in Israel. . . . Some early sketchy figures for the West Bank indicate similarly dire conditions. Four months after the start of the Intifada, West Bank gross domestic product had declined by 29 percent, individual consumption by 28 percent, and employment by 36 percent." Kimmerling and Migdal, *The Palestinian People*, 303.

30. Ibid., 300–303.

31. Sayigh, *Armed Struggle and the Search for State*, 632.

32. Kimmerling and Migdal, *The Palestinian People*, 304.

33. Barghouthi, *I Saw Ramallah*, 48.

34. Khalidi, *Palestinian Identity*, 203.

35. Hanan Ashrawi, in discussion with the author, Ramallah, August 8, 2003.

36. Palestinian Center for Policy and Survey Research, Public Opinion Poll no. 48, April 2000, http://www.pcpsr.org/survey/cprspolls/2000/poll48a.html, accessed September 2, 2003.

37. Agha and Malley, *Tragedy of Errors*, sec. 2.

38. Ashrawi, discussion.

39. Ibid.

40. Yasser Abed Rabbo, in discussion with the author, Ramallah, August 12, 2003.

41. Interim Agreement, art. 16(1).

42. Ibid., art. 17(8).

43. Ibid., annex 1, art. 9, para. 2(a).

44. Savir, *The Process*, 236.

45. Sayigh, *Armed Struggle and the Search for State*, 687 (quoting Khalid al Hassan).

46. Ibid., 689.

47. Edward Said, *The End of the Peace Process* (New York: Knopf, 2001), 98–99.

48. Sayigh, *Armed Struggle and the Search for State*, 681.

49. Abed Rabbo, discussion.

50. Yezid Sayigh, "Arafat and the Anatomy of a Revolt," *Survival* 43, no. 3 (Autumn 2001): 52.

51. Khalidi, *Palestinian Identity*, 150.

52. Sayigh, *Armed Struggle and the Search for State*, 49.

53. Abed Rabbo, discussion.

54. Kimmerling and Migdal, *The Palestinian People*, 409.

55. Ibid., 410.

56. Enderlin, *Shattered Dreams,* 234–235.

57. Senior PLO official, in discussion with the author, Ramallah.

58. Enderlin, *Shattered Dreams,* 263–264.

59. Khalidi, *Palestinian Identity,* 165–169.

60. Sayigh, *Armed Struggle and the Search for State,* 92 (quoting interview with anonymous Fateh leader).

61. Akram Hanieh, *The Camp David Papers* (Ramallah: Al Ayyam Press, 2000), 58.

62. Ashrawi, discussion.

63. Ereikat, discussion.

64. Said, *The End of the Peace Process,* 98–99.

65. Savir, *The Process,* 80.

66. Ibid., 237.

67. Interview with PLO legal adviser, Ramallah, August 7, 2003.

68. See, e.g., Savir, *The Process,* 159.

69. Ibid., 34–35.

70. See, e.g., ibid., 112 (describing how Shimon Peres dictated first draft of Taba agreement).

71. Said, *The End of the Peace Process,* 21.

72. See, e.g., Savir, *The Process,* 6 (describing conversation between Savir and Peres defining red lines for Oslo talks).

73. See, e.g., Savir, *The Process,* 103–203, 231–234.

74. Hanieh, *The Camp David Papers,* 51.

75. Agha and Malley, *Tragedy of Errors*, sec. 5.

76. Savir, *The Process,* 238.

77. Minutes of Palestinian-Israeli Negotiations, September 18, 2000 (on file with PLO Negotiations Support Unit).

78. Minutes of Palestinian-Israeli Negotiations, January 23, 2001 (on file with PLO Negotiations Support Unit).

79. Savir, *The Process,* 104.

80. Ibid., 233, 238.

81. Ibid., 231.

82. Enderlin, *Shattered Dreams,* 253.

83. Minutes of Palestinian-Israeli Negotiations, September 18, 2000 (on file with PLO Negotiations Support Unit).

84. Minutes of Palestinian-Israeli Negotiations, January 23, 2001 (on file with PLO Negotiations Support Unit).

85. Rob Malley, in discussion with the author, Washington, DC, September 4, 2003.

86. Enderlin, *Shattered Dreams,* 171.

87. Interview, PLO legal adviser.

88. Uri Savir recalls one of his first discussions with Abu Ala: "We had arrived at our first understanding. Never again would we argue about the past. This was an important step, for it moved us beyond an endless wrangle over right and wrong. Discussing the future would mean reconciling two rights, not readdressing ancient wrongs." Savir, *The Process,* 15.

89. Enderlin, *Shattered Dreams,* 202.

90. Savir, *The Process,* 104.

91. Singer, discussion.

92. Minutes of Palestinian-Israeli Negotiations, January 23, 2001 (on file with PLO Negotiations Support Unit).

93. Enderlin, *Shattered Dreams,* 209–210.

94. Akram Hanieh writes, "Opinion polls from the Gallup Institute, statements by party leaders, and articles by Israeli media commentators were more important to some in the Israeli delegation than reaching a historic peace agreement. . . . Ballot box considerations overshadowed peace considerations." Hanieh, *The Camp David Papers,* 44.

95. Interview, PLO legal adviser.

96. Aaron Miller, in discussion with the author, Washington, DC, September 2, 2003.

97. Interview, PLO legal adviser.

98. Singer, discussion.

99. Cohen, *Negotiating across Cultures,* 17.

100. Enderlin, *Shattered Dreams,* 197–198 (emphasis added).

101. Hanieh, *The Camp David Papers,* 46.

102. Agha and Malley, *Tragedy of Errors*, sec. 5.

103. Minutes of Palestinian-Israeli Negotiations, January 21, 2001 (on file with PLO Negotiations Support Unit).

104. Minutes of Palestinian-Israeli Negotiations, September 18, 2000 (on file with PLO Negotiations Support Unit).

105. Enderlin, *Shattered Dreams,* 163.

106. Gidi Grinstein, "Camp David: An Exchange," *New York Review of Books,* September 20, 2001.

107. Dennis Ross, "Camp David: An Exchange," *New York Review of Books,* September 20, 2001.

108. Ereikat, discussion.

109. Agha and Malley, *Tragedy of Errors*, sec. 5.

110. Sayigh, *Arafat and the Anatomy of a Revolt*, 53.

111. Benny Morris, "Camp David and After: An Exchange (1: An Interview with Ehud Barak)," *New York Review of Books,* June 13, 2001.

112. Khalidi, *Palestinian Identity,* 195.

4

Israeli

❖❖❖❖❖❖❖❖❖

Negotiating Culture

❖❖❖❖❖❖❖❖❖❖❖❖❖❖❖❖❖❖❖❖❖❖❖❖❖❖❖❖❖❖❖

Aharon Klieman

T his chapter outlines basic Israeli styles of negotiation in encounters with Palestinian interlocutors since 1993, during which period the Oslo initiative and open diplomatic channels have made direct communication politically acceptable. These rules of engagement are presented as external manifestations of an ongoing internal struggle for policy dominance in Jerusalem and Tel Aviv between diplomacy-oriented and security-oriented subcultures.

Of the two, it is clearly the security-oriented ethos that has prevailed for most of Israel's existence. Nevertheless, the diplomatic counter-subculture and its mindset did gain short-lived ascendance during the 1990s, when a number of prominent members of the policymaking and security establishments underwent a two-fold process of personal soul searching and socialization vis-à-vis their Palestinian counterparts that encouraged them to favor diplomatic modes of discourse. This potentially paradigmatic shift ended all too abruptly, suffering a major setback at the Camp David summit conference in July 2000, precisely when it appeared that final closure to one of the world's most enduring conflicts might be near at hand. The years since then have witnessed a sharp escalation in intercommunal violence paralleled by a de-escalation in both the frequency and substance of direct consultation between Israeli government representatives and Palestinian Authority officials.

Minding the Gap

Informing this analysis is a broader thesis about the underlying nature of the Israeli-Palestinian conflict. Arab-Jewish cultural unawareness and dismissal of "the Other" arguably played a devastating role in earlier phases of the evolving dispute; however, their explanatory power has diminished over time. To be sure, the gap between Israeli Jewish history and culture and Palestinian Arab history and culture is very real, and the reciprocal violence of recent years has done nothing to improve the situation. However, today there is a profound difference, especially for negotiation—the problem is not cultural ignorance so much as insensitivity and the refusal, knowingly, consciously, and politically, to accommodate each other's psychological needs and cultural priorities. Thus, while still present, still potent, and still poisonous, the ethnoreligious culture clash is no longer quite as compelling in accounts of exactly why it is that these two adversaries are as yet incapable of exiting their mutually hurting, mutually stifling Palestine stalemate.

This argument for subsuming cultural differences within a larger set of determinants and for assigning equal or even greater weight to other conflict variables, such as opposing political and territorial interests, challenges several pillars of conventional wisdom about the irreconcilable and immutable nature of Arab-Israeli-Palestinian relations. First, despite what commentators and propagandists would have us believe, Israelis and Palestinian Arabs are neither distant nor total strangers. Resident in suffocating proximity on the same tiny patch of land, these two ethnic, cultural, and nationalistic communities have behind them more than a century of close intercommunal encounters.[1]

Ironically enough, the two pre-intifada decades, 1967–87, featured unprecedented cultural intermingling, with Israeli consumers, children in tow, regularly marketing in towns like Qalqiliya and Tulkarem and in Jerusalem's old city, while Palestinians strolled unself-consciously in the streets of Tel Aviv and frequented Mediterranean seashore beaches. In glaring contrast, recent years have witnessed the forced and defensive reconstruction of old psychological walls of fear, insecurity, hatred, disengagement, and separation, resulting in an uneasy conflation of intimacy and estrangement in both societies. Still, the fact remains that the earlier familiarities cannot be easily or totally eradicated. Henceforth, wishing to render each other invisible or imparting to each other the worst motives become, of necessity, conscious and artificially induced acts of denial. Arabs and Jews may be estranged neighbors in Filastin/Palestine/Eretz Yisrael, but they are definitely not alien to each other.

Nor can these two Semitic peoples summarily be dismissed as social and cultural opposites. Indeed, despite the governing theme of estrangement, and without overlooking their appalling record of insensitivity, colossal misunderstandings, and spiteful working at cross-purposes, a good deal of the tragedy arises from shared commonalities, from being so much and too much alike. To be sure, strong differences and sharp asymmetries do exist, one palpable example being profoundly different tolerances toward suicidal martyrdom.[2] Yet Arabs and Jews often display strikingly similar behavior patterns and possess many of the same needs, felt insecurities, and aspirations, whether for vindication, revenge, national legitimacy and international recognition, territorial possession, physical security, or mastery over their own fate after centuries of subjugation.[3]

Nevertheless, throughout their long narrative of strife and reciprocal nonrecognition the two parties never felt either compelled or imaginative enough to engage in bargaining with, rather than battling against, each other. Not until 1993 did they achieve a minimum level of convergence by doing the hitherto unthinkable and by actually daring to engage—as equals—in direct, open discourse.

By daring throughout the nineties to step across political and psychological barriers previously thought insurmountable, Israelis and Palestinians have altered the basic equation of their relationship. As Jane Corbin noted insightfully in 1994: "More blood would yet be spilt but something fundamental had changed. The demon of hatred, fear and suspicion had been confronted, and life in that arc of land between the Mediterranean Sea and the River Jordan would never be the same."[4]

Indeed, since 1993 Israelis and Palestinians can point to more than a full decade of talking directly to and with each other. As a result, negotiations have long since explored the full range of contentious issues while delineating each party's respective nonnegotiable "red lines." But so, too, have these meetings, no matter how acrimonious at times, also fostered informality and candor touted in the scholarly literature on pacific dispute settlement as essential for promoting interpersonal working relationships, mutual respect, and degrees of trust.

This heightened awareness holds especially true for second-tier, mid-level Israeli and Palestinian officials. These "proximate policymakers,"[5] numbering twenty or so on each side, include senior advisers, civilian technocrats, functional specialists, and security experts, plus consulting academics on the periphery of negotiations, whose ongoing attendance and professional participation in joint working sessions afford not only the occasion and the channel for face-to-face conversations but also engender a sense of continuity in the dialogue.

Admittedly, these years and these political consultations show meager tangible returns if graded against the standard of a lasting accommodation, but when treated as a cumulative educational experience, they have fulfilled an indispensable function. By the mid-1990s, middle-echelon Israeli and Palestinian representatives had already taken the measure of each other's cultural and operational codes, historical narratives, and vulnerabilities. This learning process, in which wary enemy collaborators were able to explore possible understandings, to identify areas of serious disagreement as well as concurrence, and to share private confidences, has worked to soften the cultural variable's explanatory power as *the* principal determinant of the fate of Middle East conflict resolution.

Searching elsewhere for satisfactory answers to the disappointing negotiation outcome since 1993 leads us to put forward two supplemental explanations: personal and impersonal. Following seven years of intercultural exploration and exchange, when the negotiations finally seemed to be entering the closure stage at the Camp David II summit conference in July 2000, "the accident of personalities" (to borrow Henry Kissinger's phrase)[6] and the absence of interpersonal chemistry, on the one hand, combined with substantive agenda issues, on the other hand, to negate, until future notice, the progress painstakingly made at "ripening" the conflict and at spanning whatever still remains of the Israeli-Palestinian cultural divide.

Put simply, it is the profoundly complex nature of the political and territorial issues on the negotiating table—some of them all but inexplicable to outsiders—that truly bedevils the best-intentioned initiatives at peacemaking. Rather than weakening or disputing the claim for the role of culture in peacemaking, this interpretation only underlines the relevance of the cultural approach for international negotiation by incorporating *time* and *change* as independent variables. This teaches us that negative stereotypes and hate-based attitudes used in defining one's opponent, as well as self-images, are neither static nor rigid, thereby assuring that cross-cultural encounters—when Israelis meet Palestinians—are a dynamic and evolving process, both for the good and the bad. Furthermore, attitudinal change among the negotiating parties, although heartening in itself, is insufficient in moving from enmity to amity. Decision makers experiencing cultural and perceptual adjustment must take pains to bring their domestic publics along with them. Failure to do so means that rather than permeating throughout society, cultural adjustment will be confined to only a narrow strata of society, almost assuring that the change necessary for peacebuilding will be subject to backsliding and reversals at the hands of determined objectors to intercultural reconciliation.

In effect, when negotiating across cultures, learning can and does go in both directions. Cultural gaps—both those estranging individuals and those segregating entire societies—will expand and contract in response to a constant flow of environmental stimuli ranging from a single event to a pattern of words or actions emanating from one or both of the sparring partners–turned–interlocutors. In other words, we must expect to find sweeping perceptual-cultural revolutions on the scale of the 1972 United States–China rapprochement a rarity in peacemaking. Far more realistic is it to aim at building intercultural bridges incrementally, substituting goodwill for hostility through a series of measured steps. This is a fair representation of the Israeli experience and of the large, possibly overwhelming, majority of Israelis who still maintain a cautious, ambivalent view of talking peace with Palestinians.

Seven Factors Shaping Israel's Diplomatic and Negotiating Culture

Like any other diplomatic issue on Israel's national agenda, Palestinian negotiations are essentially perceived in Jerusalem and Tel Aviv through a prism comprising seven facets:

- a historical memory bank shaped by a tripartite national experience—of the Jewish people, of the Zionist enterprise, and of the state since independence in 1948—with all three elements accentuating the single overriding theme of vulnerability, conveyed most expressively by the searing Holocaust trauma that saw one-third of the Jewish people obliterated;

- the storehouse of experience in dealing with Arabs: those of British-mandated Palestine, those of the separate Arab countries, and those represented by the Palestine Liberation Organization and the Palestinian Authority;

- definitions of the national interest by civilian leaders duly vested with the political authority to prioritize national goals, supplemented by operative guidelines for the eyes of deputized negotiators detailing those tactical means best suited for advancing these larger objectives;

- an Israeli political system, in turn, whose defining features of parliamentary democracy, coalition government, and a free press largely dictate informal domestic limits to the politically and diplomatically possible;

- a pervasive defense establishment responsible for the country's military security that imposes still another informal constraint upon policy choice;

- longer-term trend and threat analyses evaluating Israel's geopolitical standing, regional and worldwide, at the moment of negotiation, as well as the perceived sense of security (or insecurity) arising from prevailing balances of power in each of the two political arenas;

- constant reassessment of the interplay of internal and external affairs at any given moment or stage of the negotiation and decisional process.

Clearly, the study of Israeli negotiating culture must begin with this seven-faced prism. It is ever present in the background to negotiation, working its subliminal effect even as the hard bargaining takes place. By the same token, we should not be surprised to discover individual members of an Israeli negotiating team, or a member of any one of the government supervisory bodies supplying official negotiating representatives with specific instructions, inserting his or her subjective reading of these seven factors. From prime minister to junior delegate, one official's confidence about Palestinian flexibility, about regional scenarios, or about overall Arab peace prospects is another's sober skepticism.

The Contending Subcultures of Israel

Researchers make the argument for culture so convincingly that the importance of cultural differences as an obstacle to be overcome in peacemaking is beyond dispute.[7] Indeed, using the idea of culture as their basic reference point, some investigators look past separate national cultures and posit the emergence under the homogenizing impact of globalization of a universal negotiating culture.[8] Leaving this debate aside and reversing direction from the general to the particular, it is important to note that "national" culture (*a* Japanese culture, *the* Russian culture), no matter how convenient a notion, is too blanket a term as well as too blunt a research tool.

Gross generalizations will simply not do, least of all in reference to a polity as open, as pluralistic, and as strongly opinionated as Israel's. There are national interests in the Israeli negotiating culture, but there are also individual, group, and institutional preferences brought into play in defining, in ranking, and in pursuing those national interests.

Anything but monolithic, a national culture really encompasses and is therefore constituted by a multiplicity of subcultures. A typical taxonomy finds a nation's *political* culture dividing into a *popular* and an *elite* political subculture, with this elite subset further deconstructing into separate *organizational* subcultures institutionalized in, represented by, and even contested by competitive bureaucratic agencies.[9] With specific reference to Israel and its political culture,[10] there are many different ways of labeling policy positions beyond the immediate and readily observable ideological dividing lines of hawk-dove, liberal-conservative, Labor-Likud.[11]

One principal dichotomy to look for in peace negotiation is one that pits a *diplomatic* subculture, with a distinctive worldview and particular set of cultural norms, premises, sensitivities, and preferences all pinned to the goal of normalized relations with the rest of the world, against a *security* subculture possessing a very different logic and orientation of its own. These two subcultures are not evenly matched. Rather, the security subculture is by far the more influential cultural subset shaping Israel's negotiating stance, because its perspective and interpretation on international, Middle Eastern, Arab, and Palestinian affairs is widely endorsed both within government circles and among the Israeli public at almost any given moment and on any national issue.[12]

Commenting on the reigning mentality governing the country's behavior shortly before Camp David II, Israeli pundit Doron Rosenblum wrote: "Look where you will these days, you will not be able to find even the trace of another narrative, an alternative opinion to that of the 'senior figures in the defense establishment,' on the coldness of their calculations, the heat of their rage, and their gang-war approach to the conflict, including vendettas and blood revenge."[13] Discounting journalistic license, Rosenblum does succeed in drawing our attention to the presence of an identifiable security subculture that in reality incorporates an even more comprehensive "political-military culture," one that colors public discussion of all policy questions, including negotiations, and that, propagated by members of Israel's sprawling defense establishment, percolates throughout society. The direct policy implication, as depicted by another leading Israeli journalist, Aluf Benn of the daily *Haaretz*, is that "Israel's policy in the conflict with the Palestinians can be summed up in ten words: 'What doesn't work with force will work with more force.'"[14]

Israel is hardly unique in possessing a security subculture,[15] but the exceptional sway this subculture has over negotiation strategy makes Israel noteworthy.[16] The primacy of national security impacts on every facet of Israeli life, from literature and cinema to the quality of life and women's rights.[17] As to what accounts for its pervasiveness, there are any number of factors, the most important of which is the unrelieved sense of existential threat to the state. Today, that threat is perceived to be posed by a spectrum of chiefly unconventional weapons, ranging from terrorist bombs to biological, chemical, and possibly even nuclear missile warheads.[18]

Unquestionably, this sense of multiple risks on multiple fronts poses an oppressive as well as constant insecurity dilemma that colors public opinion and government deliberations and that argues for sacrificing diplomatic niceties to individual and national safety in the most physical and immediate sense. As has been observed: "It is between these two symbols—between the Holocaust which befell European Jewry *and the fear of its recurrence*—that Israeli society lives."[19] The popularity of the security subculture is accentuated by a security socialization process whereby the vast majority of men and women perform national military service, followed by years of annual reserve duty, a process that renders defense both meaningful and tangible, and the security argument personal and intimate as well as overpowering.

The security subculture has engendered a vast security network, which in turn has become the subculture's chief articulator and promoter. In the Israeli context, this defense establishment encompasses not just the General Staff and the various branches of the Israel Defense Forces (IDF) but also the Ministry of Defense, the Mossad and Shabak intelligence and general security services, the National Security Council, and, not least, the defense industrial complex. Enjoying the lion's share of the national budget and unrivaled access inside the corridors of power, leading representatives of this establishment have never been celebrated for timidity in furthering their parochial institutional interests and organizational culture.[20] On the contrary, the Ministry of Defense and the General Staff of the IDF have been highly adept at parlaying the above assets into elevated status and into a correspondingly expanded definition of their assigned roles.

Despite committing a string of operational and intelligence gaffes and failing to deal conclusively with intifada-related terrorism, members of the defense-intelligence establishment nonetheless continue to speak authoritatively in diplomatic-defense matters, albeit not always with one voice. Even though their public stature has diminished in recent years owing to published media reports and official state investigatory commissions documenting their blunders, they are still respectfully listened to because "the civilian population, including cabinet members, has an instinctive tendency to view opinions proffered by intelligence experts as though they are holy writ delivered by Moses on Mount Sinai."[21]

The principal casualty of these turf wars has been the Ministry of Foreign Affairs. Long since marginalized, the ministry has been relegated to an essentially auxiliary role in implementation; it certainly does not play a vanguard role in formulating and coordinating policy on foreign and defense affairs.[22] Through a process of systematic aggrandizement, the Kirya, the sprawling Tel Aviv compound housing the headquarters of the Ministry of Defense, now enjoys enhanced and almost undivided responsibility for national intelligence assessment, policy planning, and secret diplomatic contacts as well as for arms exports and even defense ties with foreign governments. For many years, it has also been the leading bureaucratic player in all matters related to peacemaking.

Historically, the strong military presence in Israeli negotiations began with the earliest truce talks and armistice regimes that took place in 1948–49. It has continued uninterrupted, through the 1973–79 disengagement and peace talks with Egypt to the very present, in meetings with Palestinians over interim, transitional, and permanent-status arrangements for the contested West Bank and Gaza Strip territories and their inhabitants. In consequence, the lines have long since become blurred between what constitutes defense and what constitutes foreign affairs, making references to a fairly integrated Israeli "political-military culture" possible. It is small wonder, therefore, that leading defense actors have insinuated themselves successfully into all political negotiations undertaken by Israel with the Palestinians, barring the single most notable exception: the secret Oslo channel that yielded the 1993 Declaration of Principles. Moreover, they tend not only to participate in but to chair or cochair Israeli peace delegations, to set agendas, and to control the overall tenor of the discussions.

The Safety-First Approach

What constitutes this Israeli security culture? For one thing, it represents an entire Israeli mindset, offering a comprehensive geopolitical outlook and worldview. This security culture both poses fundamental questions and provides unambiguous answers about issues such as the conduct of world politics and the nature of relations between the Jewish state and non-Jewish nations, as well as the nature and uses of national power.

First principles include an assumed anarchic Hobbesian international system; an abiding suspicion concerning the willingness of the international community and of the Arab-Islamic world to grant the Jewish state and the Jewish people full acceptance; a belief in the absolute necessity for preserving a self-help and self-defense capacity against all threats based upon deterrent military power, and the will to use that power when and where necessary; and a built-in prejudice against theorizing and against long-range strategic planning matched by a very deep, very strong institutionalized bias in favor of dealing with the short-term and with immediate, sudden contingencies.

This entire line of reasoning, with its emphasis on toughness in an unforgiving Middle Eastern neighborhood and a cynical world, which many experts trace to the formative experience in the struggle for statehood and to the deep imprint of David Ben-Gurion, Israel's first premier (*and* defense minister!), lies at the heart of the Israeli military ethos. Inculcated in successive generations of army commanders, it permeates both sectors of the defense establishment, civilian and military.

However, Israeli security thinking is far more inclusive, extending beyond the first principles to cover topics such as how one enters, interprets, and conducts negotiation. Such thinking bears on basic attitudes toward the Arabs as negotiating partners. It affects matters of style, deportment, and temperament in deliberating with Egyptians, Jordanians, Lebanese, Syrians, and Palestinians. It also has an important bearing on the group dynamic taking place within Israeli negotiating teams and on civilian-military relations in general.[23]

The Meaning and Uses of Negotiation

Immersed in the teachings of Carl von Clausewitz, ranking IDF officers will readily quote his famous dictum that "war is simply a continuation of political intercourse, with the addition of other means," which serves as the leitmotif for his 1832 classic study, *On War*.[24] Schooled in war as an instrument of policy, they are inclined to see the proceedings through the narrow eye of security once they are thrust into negotiating situations, with each prospective move—theirs and the opponent's—appraised as either security imperiling or security enhancing.

Befitting a professional military ethos, Israeli soldiers-turned-diplomats retain their propensity for favoring the use of force even when waging peace. Quick military solutions to political problems or threats are preferable to grinding diplomatic exercises. Should negotiation prove inconclusive and persuasion unsatisfactory, the iron fist remains, alternatively, Israel's first choice or default option in the defense of national security.

Especially if Israel is considered to be negotiating from strength, these soldiers in mufti are prone to treating diplomatic talks as analogous to wars of attrition, and therefore to be conducted in either of two modes: as a game of waiting out the opponent or as a lightning offensive aimed at breaking the back of resistance. If the former, then the objective is to wear down one's adversary in a battle of wills through such stratagems as looking for the tactical high ground, refusing to budge, and fighting for every inch by wrangling over what might appear to outsiders to be technical, even trivial, details. If the latter, then the enemy's bargaining position is best taken by storm, using intimidation and bluff: assume neither goodwill nor magnanimity on the part of Arab opponents; present maximum demands (and anticipate your opponent doing likewise) in the knowledge one can always back down and offer concessions, especially symbolic ones, further along in the negotiation; bring constant pressure to bear; if warranted, apply steadily mounting pressure in constantly devising and tabling fresh counterproposals; insist upon quid pro quo; and outsmart the opposing side by probing for openings, soft spots, and weaknesses.

Negotiating with Arabs

The security culture further posits that in negotiation, as in field combat, the art of survival for a small, isolated, and outnumbered state lies in ceaseless maneuver and in the timeless ploy of *divide et impera*. Applied in a Middle Eastern context, the politics of divide and rule have always argued for splitting the larger enemy Arab coalition, hence Israel's decades-long tacit alliance with the Hashemite Kingdom of Jordan against Palestinian aspirations; its successful efforts to disengage Egypt from the Arab resistance front; and its eagerness to get Yasser Arafat and the Palestine Liberation Organization (PLO) to commit themselves on paper in 1993 to a negotiated compromise settlement in defiance of Syria and other holdout Arab countries. This goal of exploiting Arab disunity and centrifugal forces within the Islamic world is a keystone of the security approach carried over into negotiation. It helps explain the unambiguous preference by Jerusalem for a bilateral framework over the multilateral and comprehensive "roundtable" format favored by Arab and Palestinian strategists as a way of outnumbering, isolating, and then pressuring Israel by inviting outside international intervention. A perfect example is the tactical, psychological, and bargaining advantage of playing Syrians against Palestinians when weighing fresh peace options for Jerusalem. Should an Israeli government be of a frame of mind to signal its willingness in principle to re-open negotiation, by using the argument of being unable to conduct two negotiating tracks simultaneously and, domestically, unable to make painful concessions on both fronts, Israel has the latitude of choosing which of the two rival parties it prefers in signaling the better deal.

Other defense establishment biases revolve around an essentially cynical image of the Arabs: as respecting power and understanding the language of force, as duplicitous, as untrustworthy. Indeed, Israeli security culture and the security experience are encapsulated in a play on one of the more quotable aphorisms coined by U.S. president Ronald Reagan: "Verify, and

Don't Trust!" The same cold realism and misgivings lead security experts to insist that in any negotiated arrangement security must rest solely and directly in Israel's hands; that an imposed settlement from outside, whatever the source and whoever the guarantor, must be resisted; that any outside international presence in implementing a settlement must be minimal; and that there can be no appeasing Arabs, given their own cultural lenses that cause them to misinterpret concessions as a sign of weakness and lack of resolve on Israel's part, thereby achieving the least desirable bargaining outcome of only whetting an opponent's appetite for still further unilateral concessions by Israel.

Negotiating with Palestinians

Dealing specifically with Palestinians accentuates many of these security-derived images and tactics. In defense establishment thinking, it is they, the Palestinians, as the weaker, more dependent side, who ought to be pressed and who should be yielding ground, backing down, and making deadlock-breaking concessions. Even allowing for a positive Israeli learning curve, attitudes toward PLO and Palestinian Authority officials still tend to fall somewhere between condescension and poorly concealed contempt for low levels of professionalism.[25] Certainly, the professional military respect shown Egyptian and Jordanian commanders is usually absent when Israeli officers deal with Palestinian security personnel, and wariness toward Arabs in general reaches new heights whenever Palestinian motives, intentions, sincerity, flexibility, and enforcement capabilities are evaluated. The fact that the Palestinian camp comprises disparate constituent parts encourages Israel to use divide-and-rule tactics, looking for discord within the rival delegation by playing to the vanities, jealousies, and ambitions of its members: splitting Gazans from West Bankers, Fateh from non-Fateh, pragmatists from hard-liners; Arafat loyalists from dissenters; and the old guard from the new guard of younger hawkish street fighters and aspiring newcomers eager to make a name for themselves politically.

Bargaining Behavior

Members of the defense establishment seconded to Israeli negotiating teams outwardly display certain attributes that, while more tendency and esprit than army code, and not without exception, do come close to qualifying as shared security subculture traits. Palestinian, Arab, European, American, and UN participants in security talks are known to comment, not uncritically, about this stylistic side of negotiating, and about three mannerisms in particular: impatience, swagger, and instrumentalism.

Although able to turn on the charm when they wish to, Israeli generals, in uniform or out, are just as often noted for their undiplomatic bluntness (known in Hebrew as *dugri*) and for their tough talk at the negotiating table. Prized in Israeli society and culture, such businesslike directness *(tachlis)* can easily be interpreted as offensive when equated with insolence and disrespect in Arab-Palestinian culture, and can seem a breach of etiquette in the eyes of third-party professional diplomatists for whom formalities, patience, pleasantries, and courtesies—not to mention long-winded statements for the record devoid of any real practical substance—are an integral part of the structured negotiation process.

Taught to think spur of the moment and short term, and to zero in on facts on the ground, ranking and former military officers understandably have a hard time adjusting to a world of diplomatic protocol and, in their eyes, stilted bargaining procedures—hence, their show at times of demonstrative impatience with political niceties and endless palaver and with judgmental, fickle world opinion, ritualistic UN resolutions, and legal casuistry. Tactically, on the other hand, once having tabled for the official record specific security desiderata at the Cairo (1994), Washington (1995), and Wye River (1998) negotiations over further interim agreements, spokesmen for the military point of view then deferred to legal experts in the delegation to sew matters up by inscribing with elaborate care and in painstaking detail the necessary security provisions against virtually every conceivable potential threat scenario.

Equally intimidating to nonmilitary negotiators on the opposite side of the table is the air of self-assurance security types might often project. Field commanders are steeped in Israeli military traditions that include, inter alia, being quick studies in taking charge, relying on personal judgment, seizing the initiative, and going on the offensive. Moreover, IDF professional soldiers enter Middle East security and peace talks armed with tools that bespeak their expert grasp of the situation: impressive charts, maps, data-filled spreadsheets, and PowerPoint presentations. This assertiveness leaves a fine line to be walked in negotiating situations between quiet self-confidence in one's expertise and grasp of detail while speaking with authority, on the one hand, and, on the other, conveying a sense of overbearing arrogance and superiority.

A third characteristic of those with a strong security background is instrumentalism. Products of Israeli's security subculture tend to show little respect for momentary goodwill gestures and for what are commonly referred to as the "atmospherics" of peacemaking; confident that Israel is the stronger side, they also see no reason to be unnecessarily forthcoming. When negotiations are at an impasse and the level of Palestinian violence escalates, this instrumentalism translates into a readiness to use strong retaliatory coercive measures. Conversely, what in principle may make military negotiators more amenable to trade-offs is the absence of any deep sentimental attachment toward, for example, the West Bank cradle of Jewish history and civilization or Jerusalem's Temple Mount.

In effect, the contested territories of Judea and Samaria are perceived of as little more than bargaining chips to be used in bartering for security tangibles—demilitarization, the right to conduct aerial reconnaissance over Palestinian airspace, listening posts in the Jordan Valley, and the like—or in trade for security increments in the form of military hardware and military funding, possibly even a mutual security pact with the United States.[26] In all likelihood this philosophy of pragmatism is what has enabled defense veterans such as Amnon Lipkin-Shahak and Ami Ayalon to find common cause in recent years with dovish initiatives predicated upon "land for peace," with peace rather than defense perimeters in turn represented as the ultimate guarantor of security. This is an important point, for if validated it corresponds to the kind of reasoning employed across the Israeli subcultural divide by diplomatists and enthusiasts for negotiation.

The Diplomatic Counterculture

Eliot Cohen, quoting de Gaulle on a military temperament "bred on imperatives," notes how "taste for system . . . self-assurance and . . . rigidity" are inbred in the soldier. Such a mindset sets the stage for a sharp clash within society between civilian and military cultures: "Everything in the military code which is absolute, peremptory, and not to be questioned is repugnant to those who live in a world of rough and ready solutions, endless intriguing, and decisions which may be reversed at a moment's notice."[27] Mistrust of politicians and diplomats by generals, and of generals by politicians and diplomats certainly finds ample expression in the competition over the ruling Israeli negotiating culture.

Part of this traces to professional military inbreeding and an IDF esprit de corps tested under fire that encourages confidence in comrades-in-arms holding a shared ethos and a grammar of their own (but that does not preclude intriguing and backbiting among them). Still another source for the mistrust lies in the noticeable lack of confidence and esteem for the two main subgroups—politicians and career diplomats—customarily mandated to negotiate in Israel's name with Arabs, Palestinians, and third-party intermediaries.

While defense establishment personnel and IDF officers duly acknowledge (although not necessarily always respect) civilian superiority, they also possess their own toolbox of subtle and less subtle ways for either circumventing or countering formal government controls. Defense ministers, many of them former army careerists, and determined chiefs of staff have been known to pursue parallel, outflanking initiatives in the midst of negotiations or to force the suspension of those talks. They have also acted as an advocacy and pressure group, lobbying from within, mobilizing public opinion, leaking to the media, and steamrolling decision making in the cabinet.

Yoram Peri convincingly traces how one unit, the Strategic Planning Division of the IDF General Staff, gradually inserted itself into the actual political process after 1969 as the long arm of the military. More recently, when Prime Minister Binyamin Netanyahu took office in 1996 he may have believed it unhealthy for IDF top brass to rub shoulders with Israel's adversaries at diplomatic conferences and cocktail receptions, but he soon came to appreciate that without the military he and his government lacked the ability to conduct complicated political-security negotiations.[28] This realization left him no choice but to reinsert IDF officers into the negotiating process. Over this same time span, the Foreign Ministry became accustomed to see its departmental stand overridden by the sheer weight of the security argument or, worse, its personnel uninvited to participate even in pre-decisional policy consultations.

Such behavior may be endemic to intramural bureaucratic wars but it is accentuated by Israeli politics. As an identifiable subgroup, the military tend to be judgmental, finding fault among national leaders, and even fellow officers, as well as among Arabs in general and Palestinians in particular. As an in-group they share a disparaging view of "outsider" Israeli government figures, Knesset members, and Israeli diplomats, characterized —off the record—by such epithets as "compromisers," "vacillators," and, deepest cut of all, "appeasers" and *"politikai'im"* (crass politicians).

In contrast to the security subculture, political leaders do tend to think in more encompassing political terms. Their definition of the national interest is broader, taking into consideration needs and policies besides defense. They are very much attuned to the mood of the country, the Knesset, their party, and their coalition partners in considering negotiation options. Nor would they be reticent in confessing to a desire to retain popularity and stay in power. Having accepted ultimate responsibility for walking the thinnest of high wires in attempting to achieve equilibrium between peacemaking and security under circumstances of peril and uncertainty for Israel, they constantly dread stumbling disastrously. How could they not? In short, for them expediency is not a dirty word.

Much the same holds true for diplomats and their diplomatic culture. From their perspective Israel's present and longer-term security is intimately tied up with the country's international stature, its global reputation and image abroad. Security in the larger sense is ultimately pegged on achieving peaceful settlement and normalized relations with the Jewish state's immediate Arab and Muslim neighbors. Cardinal for both the peace and the security of Israel are maintaining close and cordial relations with the United States, cementing kinship bonds to world Jewry, strengthening ties with the European Union, NATO, and the Afro-Asian countries of the Third World, and reengaging the United Nations as a contributing member in good standing. For all of these goals, the prerequisite is a satisfactory end to the Middle East conflict, widely regarded as the primary cause of Israel's isolation and alienation.

This, plus the diplomatic ethos of persuasion and tact, puts a premium on great patience and great sensitivity in talks with Arab representatives. For the trained diplomat, all negotiation, but especially dispute resolution, represents a protracted, even tedious process, a process calling for more than a modicum of goodwill and generosity, for listening carefully to adversaries and their concerns, for legal formulas and formulations, for symbolic gestures, and for concessions and mutual, not necessarily reciprocal, compromises.

Diplomatic codes of conduct are antithetical to the professional ethos of the defense establishment, with the resultant clash clearly reflected in the two contrasting approaches to negotiation. Israel, as both the perceived and the statistically more powerful player, claim the statesmen, should show generosity of spirit; Israel need not be forthcoming, protest their security counterparts, especially when unilateral concessions are seized upon in Arab culture as evidence of diminished staying power. What matters in statesmanship, say the former, is the ability to rise above the immediate situation; no, insist the latter, the only thing that matters is the concrete situation immediately at hand.

Besides contrasting the two dichotomous Israeli negotiating subcultures, it is useful but also necessary to blur the lines by weaving negotiating personalities into the discussion. To be sure, one possible grouping of Israeli bargainers remains also the most straightforward, pitting civilians opposed to the military interpretation of security as altogether too confining and narrow against the security establishment; diplomatists versus the generals. Famous examples include the late Abba Eban, and Yossi Beilin, first entrant into the Oslo channel, neither of whom enjoyed any standing or respect in the defense establishment nor claimed any pretenses about sharing its worldview. Another, more recent, figure is Shlomo Ben-Ami, a professor of history, foreign minister, and principal negotiator under Prime Minister Ehud Barak, whose rise to prominence within the Labor Party came after a celebrated stint as Israel's first ambassador to Spain. In his anxious efforts to do something at the 2000 summit, amply documented in his own account of the proceedings during and after Camp David II, Ben-Ami was personally instrumental in tabling supplemental concessions that in effect systemically erased Israeli "red lines" meant to be held fast in bargaining opposite the Palestinians.[29]

Less readily obvious, though, is a second grouping of individuals, who authenticate that for all its formidability the defense establishment subculture is by no means monolithic. Even among cabinet-level leaders labeled *bitchonistim* ("security firsters"), there can be significant differences between those who reach top government positions through a career trajectory as graduates of the IDF and those whose ascent owes nothing to formal military service in the IDF. Shimon Peres and Moshe Arens— both of them defense ministers—showcase instances of national leaders whose résumés highlight long, meritorious service in the Kirya but who never gained full acceptance from quintessential IDF insiders such as former chiefs of staff Moshe Dayan, Yitzhak Rabin, and Ehud Barak.

Singularly noteworthy as a third category are the nonconformists: those representatives of the military ethos who have dared to break ranks, converting from hawkish to dovish positions precisely over questions of whether and how to talk to the Palestinians. One of the first was a former head of military intelligence, the late Professor Yehoshafat Harkabi, then followed by Moshe Dayan, who brought his no-nonsense pragmatism to bear at the first Camp David summit in 1978 in saving the trilateral Israel-U.S.-Egypt talks from ending acrimoniously, and by former air force commander Ezer Weizman, who resigned as minister of defense under Prime Minister Menachem Begin in anger over Likud cabinet intransigence and insensitivity toward Cairo. Joining them in this third rubric is Yitzhak Rabin. The same Yitzhak Rabin who, after having responded to the first intifada uprising in 1987 by instructing the army to "go in and break some bones," committed himself, and Israel, in 1993 to negotiating in good faith with the Palestinians—a transition confirmed for us by Arafat himself in extolling the late Israeli leader's courage in partnering the 1993 peace initiative.

In terms of strict adherence versus adaptation and change on the part of career specialists otherwise pigeonholed and stereotyped by professional subculture, the above-mentioned Israelis highlight the weakness, indeed the danger, in assuming "once a general, always a general." From De Gaulle to Rabin, the history of peace breakthroughs either stimulated by or stimulants for intercultural sensitivity confirms that the warrior-statesman is as much a reality as it is an ideal type of leadership.

When analysis shifts to the different rounds of peace talks engaged in by Israeli delegations with Arab and Palestinian leaders, this special form of cultural fault line—not between Arabs and Jews but among Israelis themselves—has important consequences for Israeli patterns of negotiating behavior.

Getting to Know You: When Israelis Meet Arabs

If ever two negotiating sides lacked the rudimentary skills needed for facilitating conversational learning in instances of intercultural engagement it was Israelis and Palestinian Arabs. In the throes of their all-consuming "one long war,"[30] they had managed by the end of the 1980s to convince themselves—and each other—that not all wars must end. Accustomed to living in conditions of extreme enmity and in a region where compassion is often scorned as cultural deformity, both sides approached anything hinting at official contact with the greatest hesitancy and caution.[31] And yet, despite such inauspicious circumstances, the two parties would go on to launch a dual process of negotiation and learning, at first secret, then open and formal.

In the early 1990s a handful of Israelis willing to assume the risks arising whenever enemies dare shift from habituated inaction to initiative took the first measured steps in feeling their way to prenegotiation. In this phase leading up to Oslo, these early believers in the potential of a Palestinian option for Israel and for peace prospects enjoyed one marked advantage: the ability to draw from a rich database of accumulated experience in previously facing Arab representatives.[32] Fifteen years of negotiating openly with Egyptians plus forty-five years of clandestine working relations with the innermost circle of King Hussein's palace guard and with the Jordanian monarch himself had taught Israelis that cooperation could be achieved by developing trust, by displaying sensitivity toward the premium Arab culture puts upon saving face, and by listening reflectively to each other's deepest concerns. The lessons learned in these sustained encounters were supplemented over the years by experiences gained from a network of bilateral contacts with the governments and cultures of Lebanon, Morocco, and Syria.

This meant that many of the painful prenegotiation and negotiation learning preliminaries—such as feeling at ease in the presence of one's arch enemies, probing their intentions, testing one's own prejudices against their behavior and responses, and then revising stereotypes in light of those responses—had already been undertaken, and weathered, by seasoned diplomats in Jerusalem, leading to a substantially revised Israeli handbook on Arabs and Arab political culture. Techniques employed and lessons learned, many of them sobering, contributed to a more honest and balanced approach to Middle East negotiation and to greater realism about what could and could not be achieved in Israeli-Arab intercultural negotiating dynamics.

However, when Israel finally found itself poised on the brink of negotiations with Palestinians in 1993, nothing of Israel's cumulative experience with other Arab countries or acquired respect for rulers such as Anwar Sadat, King Hassan II of Morocco, and the Hashemites' King Hussein and his brother Prince Hassan very much mattered. Israelis traditionally and overwhelmingly viewed the Palestinians, the PLO, and Arafat as anathema. The Palestinians were a non-nation; the PLO was a terrorist organization; and Arafat was an "obscene slaughterer of innocents"[33] to be held in justified contempt. As Uri Savir comments in his personal account of Israel's first encounters with the Palestinians in the Oslo channel, few negotiations in modern diplomatic history have been launched in the context of so adversarial a relationship.[34]

But then a three-part reassessment began to gain endorsement in Jerusalem. It was recognized, first, that mainstream Israelis were ready to consider lowering mental and cultural barriers long ago erected against the existence and plight of the Palestinians and of their national distinctiveness in much the same way that most Israelis had previously revised their negative attitudes toward Egyptians; second, that the Palestinians were likewise trying to overcome their own cultural demons; and third, that reciprocal confidence-building measures were starting to have precisely the desired dual effect of enabling official negotiators to relate to each other with greater cultural familiarity and, as a result, to progress toward additional political understandings with increased public backing.

Once launched, the dual education-negotiation process did begin to make significant inroads in terms of Israeli thinking. "Shaking hands and building a partnership," remarked Savir, "meant not only the renunciation of past hostility but a break with traditions deeply ingrained in each of our societies."[35] One of the more colorful illustrations he offers has two prominent representatives of the Israeli defense establishment, Deputy Chief of Staff Amnon Lipkin-Shahak and Ya'akov Perry, director of the General Security Services, conducting security talks over the course of several weeks in late 1993 with the designated Palestinian heads of Preventive Security in Gaza and Jericho, Mohammad Dahlan and Jibril Rajoub, both of whom had spent years in Israeli prisons. Thanks to the Palestinians' ability to curb their residual resentment, and to the Israelis avoiding any hint of condescension, the four men succeeded in forming a "backslapping relationship marked by gruff humor" made so special by "their common mastery of a language of force, tempered by human sympathy."[36]

A still more powerful if not altogether representative example of rapport is Savir's own personal relationship with his opposite number, Ahmed Qurei (also known as Abu Ala), which extended at times to bantering and to developing a private lexicon of jokes. In a particularly poignant thumb-nail sketch of the sensitive Oslo proceedings, Savir captures the profound uncertainty associated with such cultural transformations. Of the negotiations, he writes:

> Conducted with great intensity for fifty hours or more at a time, with breaks only for two or three hours' sleep and a hearty Norwegian meal, they resembled a marathon chess game fraught with feints, bluffs, and diversions. The confrontations were often brutal, the crises close to shattering. Sometimes the tensions broke in near-hysterical laughter; sometimes we pushed each other almost to the point of rage. The emotional outbursts in those sessions buffeted us between hatred and empathy. It was as if all we had felt toward each other in the past, and all we were hoping to feel in the future, gushed out to swamp us in ambivalence, on the passage from rejection to compromise.[37]

He adds, "Most surprising to me were the many defenses we shared: suspicion, cynicism, defensive humor, deep feelings of historical deprivation."

To be sure, this should not be misinterpreted as meaning the embryonic cross-cultural understanding diffused uniformly across both camps, or that Israel's entire political elite embraced it. With few exceptions, the willingness to refit cultural lenses did not reach as far up as the highest national leaders—the "Summiteers," who do not as a matter of both protocol and routine participate on a regular basis in direct encounters with Palestinians. Of the prime ministers and foreign ministers holding office in the decade from 1990 to 2000, Shimon Peres and Shlomo Ben-Ami were the most amenable to the idea of revising their opinions of the Palestinians; Yitzhak Shamir, Binyamin Netanyahu, and Ariel Sharon the least disposed; and Yitzhak Rabin positioned near the center, disinclined yet willing to be convinced.

Enigmatic is the only way to categorize the attitude of Prime Minister Ehud Barak. Among the more outspoken early critics of the Oslo Accords when he was chief of staff in 1993, by the close of the decade he had come to accept the principle of Palestinian statehood, and as premier in 1999 declared: "To our Palestinian neighbors, I say in all sincerity: We want to work with your leaders, first and foremost Yasser Arafat, in full partnership and respect, in order to assure a hopeful, free and prosperous future for the coming generations which will live alongside each other in this land."[38] When asked in a television interview what he might have done had he been born a Palestinian, Barak confessed, "I would probably have joined a terrorist organization."[39] If truly indicative, all of this suggests that in terms of understanding, empathy, and compromise, Barak had made his own personal peace with the Palestinians, if only as the vehicle necessary for realizing the original Zionist dream of Jewish normalcy. It is also then easier to understand why he promoted the Camp David summit meeting so aggressively during the first half of 2000, looking to bypass further interim-phase negotiations and move directly to resolve final-status issues in the belief that an end-of-conflict accord was within reach.

Once encamped at Camp David, however, he then exhibited behavior patterns at odds with any standard menu for cultural bridging. Distant, brooding, suspicious, and overbearing, Barak actually succeeded in matching Arafat in peevishness. What makes his outer petulance the more perplexing is its striking contrast to the far more forthcoming stance he was prepared to show on matters of principle and substance, most notably, on the depth of Israel's withdrawal, almost back to the 1967 armistice lines, and his consent, in defiance of what until 2000 had been the national consensus, to dividing Jerusalem with Arafat's Palestinian Authority. His demeanor also stands in stark contrast to the propensity for adjusting cultural filters among those on the Israeli teams charged with actually handling the ongoing negotiations at the various meetings, seminars, and workshops constituting the follow-up to Oslo.

Proximity Talks

Unlearning may be no less important than learning in achieving cultural fluency. Those seven interim years from Oslo to Camp David constituted an invaluable political, social, and cultural laboratory. Among the Israeli regulars were people such as Beilin and Savir, Lipkin-Shahak, Ron Pundak, Yoel Singer, Avi Gil, Dan Meridor, Yitzhak Molcho, Danny Naveh, Oded Eran, Ami Ayalon, Gilead Sher, General Shlomo Yanai, and Colonel Shaul Arieli, often replacing each other as team leaders and delegates, plus a substantially larger number of lower-ranking economic, security, and technical specialists. Joining them from the Palestinian side were such fixtures as Abu Ala, Dahlan, and Rajoub, Mahmoud Abbas (also known as Abu Mazen), Nabil Sha'ath, Hassan Asfour, Yasser Abed Rabbo, Muhammad Rashid, and Ziad Abu Zayyad, augmented by a support team of functional specialists. Together these peace processors wrote a new page—more like a first draft, really—in the theory of social psychology and social learning theory as applied to conflict resolution.

Coined "the Oslo spirit," this bridging process never for a moment eradicated residual suspicions and prejudices in either the Israeli or the Palestinian camp. Each side reserved, and exercised, the right to retain lingering misgivings about the true extent of the other's commitment to a workable peace. As a consequence, mutual testing coincided with the mutual building of rudimentary trust in a mottled pattern of "soft" learning and "hard" bargaining.

As intelligence profiles assumed flesh-and-blood personality, what had begun modestly with conscious efforts by both delegations not to offend slowly ratcheted up—from alienation avoidance to gestures of a more positive and constructive nature. While one should be wary of imparting excessive importance to personalized diplomacy, it is significant that in several cases working relationships developed into personal ones as regular attendees, thrust by negotiating logistics into sharing coffee breaks as well as traveling, dining, and even duty-free shopping together, gradually came to feel comfortable in one another's company.

Still, the format of periodic but face-to-face negotiation in theory merely creates the occasion for ongoing contacts in multiple diplomatic channels. Of far greater significance is the fact that the widening in-groups of second-level Israeli and Palestinian negotiators who conducted the ongoing talks (the "Regulars") did actually form, as it were, a league of pragmatists who, in turn, utilized opportunities for talking directly to put together an unwritten set of shared rules of behavior. These rules then made it possible for Israeli and Palestinian representatives to join in the larger search for cultural commonalities and to be respectful of the other side even as they continued to fight fiercely over individual procedural and substantive agenda details. Testifying to the strength of this Oslo spirit, one of the young lawyers seconded to the Palestinian Negotiation Support Unit recalled how as late as July 2000, while Barak and Arafat were going at each other tooth and nail, he still got along well with the Israeli legal team at Camp David because "we could speak the same language, literally and figuratively; we shared the same cultural cues."[40]

Israeli Regulars similarly came to feel a sense of responsibility for seeing the original Oslo gamble through to successful completion by using this new language of discourse in order to surmount differences and facilitate

pragmatic problem solving. Experiences both across and behind the negotiating table, and in a steady round of dialoguing and conferencing through
the medium of track-two diplomacy, encouraged a tendency on both sides
to push ahead on interim-phase negotiations, to emphasize the positive, to
defer intractable issues, and to gloss over the other side's infractions. One
telling instance concerned the number of authorized Palestinian Authority security personnel in uniform and under arms, and the number and
caliber of their weapons. In the face of continuing violations by the Palestinian Authority of the ceilings agreed upon in the 1995 Interim Agreement, Israeli officials were content to register verbal and written protesta-
tions, while others readily accepted Palestinian justifications, such as the
need for arming and employing larger numbers of salaried recruits in
order for Arafat to be seen as distributing tangible benefits to his people,
and to enforce law and order in those areas of Gaza and the West Bank
only recently entrusted to him.

Both in-groups found it necessary to persevere in the face of sustained
criticism from detractors at home who were bitterly opposed to compromise peacemaking in any form or who, at a minimum, insisted upon holding the other party strictly accountable to the letter of the Oslo, Cairo, and
Washington agreements. These Regulars also felt the need to persist in
the face of immediate political superiors too shortsighted, too intimidated,
or too ideological to sanction the political concessions necessary for sus-
taining momentum. Herein lay the rationale for a remarkable realignment,
broadly speaking—setting off, on the one side, Israeli and Palestinian
Regulars from, on the other side, Israeli and Palestinian Summiteers. The
former were less prone to resort to brinkmanship, to fabricating crises,
and to threats, bluffs, or blackmail tactics that remained the stock in trade
of the Summiteers.

Convinced of the wisdom of keeping the ball in play, Israeli Regulars
were usually the ones found urging decision makers in Jerusalem to consider not one but two sets of interests, and they would continually devise
practical ways for resolving each impasse du jour as it arose. One preferred
stratagem readily at the disposal of Israeli tacticians resolved to push forward was to engage their opposite numbers in a conspiracy not of silence
but of imprecision. Better known in diplomatic and negotiation parlance
as ambiguity—or, in variant form, as "constructive ambiguity"[41]—this
negotiating technique frequently served the Regulars well in getting from

the Norway channel to Camp David. As Abu Ala confided to Yossi Beilin very early in the process, insistence upon premature clarification of all points was liable to prolong the negotiations and delay implementation of the interim agreements, whereas vagueness in the declaration of principles, Abu Ala observed, need not be necessarily negative, but a means for leaving the two sides free to interpret agreements in the manner best suited to their respective domestic requirements, thus keeping the door open to further rounds of negotiation.[42]

From the perspective of intercultural negotiation, the beauty of constructive ambiguity for the negotiator lies in its manifold virtues—at least over the short term. Convenient for defusing crises, it is premised upon finding momentary working solutions.[43] It is therefore the handmaid of gradualism and the step-by-step approach to peacemaking, best suited for putting off for as long as politically possible the truly contentious issues. So, too, does ambiguity encourage cultural sensitivity and diplomatic creativity in trying to avoid embarrassment whenever one or both sides may be called upon to make painful unilateral concessions, to compromise principles, or to sacrifice self-respect. Not the least of its appeal is that skillful application of imprecise yet mutually acceptable wording formulas helps convey the impression of progress on what remain at heart (and what are known to the negotiators, Regulars and Summiteers alike, to be) extraordinarily intractable issues. Less underscored both by enthusiasts for ambiguity in negotiation and by the Middle East negotiators themselves, devising loopholes instead of confronting hard-core issues forthrightly also supplied both sides with the convenient pretext for breaching signed accords.

Thanks to proximity, dialogue, and intentionally ambiguous, watereddown terminology, the end of the 1990s seemed to indicate that the remaining bilateral Israeli-Palestinian cultural divide was being done away with. Certainly this was the prevailing surface impression, so that when cushioning his deep personal disappointment at the failure of Camp David II, President Bill Clinton could still underscore the positive: "Let me give you some good news: Of all the peace groups I've ever worked with, these people know each other, they know the names of each other's children, they know how many grandchildren the grandparents have, they know their life stories, they have a genuine respect and understanding for each other."[44] Lest there be any doubt, Clinton's complimentary reference was to the Regulars, not to Summiteers Arafat and Barak.

Which poses the telling question: from an Israeli cultural perspective, after such sustained efforts at lowering psychological and cultural barriers, why did the follow-up stage to the 1993–2000 interim negotiating-learning process finish so badly? How is it that Camp David II, intended to be the endgame in Israeli-Palestinian conflict termination and reconciliation, is recalled today as a stinging diplomatic failure, as well as a resounding setback for Israel's revised peace strategy?

The Blame Game, or Getting to No You

Commentaries about responsibility for "that miserable summit" held between July 11 and 25, 2000, in the secluded Catoctin Mountains continue to be printed, supplemented by personalized, behind-the-scenes accounts by direct participants on what really went wrong. Palestinian negotiator Saeb Ereikat, however, remains in a minority of one in risibly suggesting Camp David was actually a success, and that Clinton, Arafat, and Barak "should be congratulated for having brought us so close."[45] If we recognize the summit for what it was, a diplomatic calamity—at least from Israel's standpoint—and if we confine our search for explanations of the summit's failure to the cultural sphere, three alternative interpretations present themselves.

- *Positive Convergence.* Many of the previous efforts and gestures by Israelis toward better understanding had been reciprocated by the Palestinians, and each side had undertaken meaningful cultural adjustments and was committed to making more in a joint campaign aimed at reducing to an absolute minimum the detrimental influence of intercultural misperception—only to have culture once again trumped by character and by politics at Camp David.

- *Negative Asymmetry.* The Oslo signing, the handshake on the White House lawn, and the Nobel Peace Prize ceremonies had been little more than a sham. The Palestinian camp had never really become attuned to Jewish nationalism's deepest longing for normalcy. Key figures in the Israeli political establishment, from Rabin, Peres, and Beilin down, may have progressed in their learning curve, but their earnestness went unreciprocated. Accordingly, Camp David exposed two failings: a veteran Palestinian leadership still mired in self-pity and in denial of the

Jewish state's legitimacy;[46] and an Israeli policy seriously flawed by self-deception and by wishful thinking in projecting the same good faith effort onto the Palestinians. In support of this view, political scientist Shlomo Avineri in 2002 described Israelis and Palestinians as finding themselves "exactly where they started: Facing one another across an abyss of irreconcilable differences."[47] Even Shlomo Ben-Ami, a direct participant in both the Camp David and later Taba meetings, asked in frustration, "Tell me what more we were supposed to do?" In an audible note of disillusionment he was forced to conclude that the Palestinians "don't want a solution as much as they want to place Israel in the dock of the accused" as part of their unwavering goal of "undermining our existence as a Jewish state."[48]

• *Negative Divergence*. The cultural barriers erected on *both* sides had not really been lowered, let alone removed, during the preceding seven years of negotiations. These barriers may, in fact, have been unassailable, and each side's sense of its status as underdog and victim too self-reassuring to be relinquished. Alternatively, Israelis and Palestinians may have been engaging in a cynical masquerade of deception and deceit, wishing only to create the impression of enlightened realism without actually intending to acknowledge wrongdoing or to execute deepseated political and cultural adjustments. Camp David II finally exposed the duplicitous game played by the two antagonists.

Many outside observers may choose, in the name of evenhandedness, to adopt the third interpretation of Camp David II's failure, apportioning the blame equally. Most Israelis, however, bolstered by independent public opinion surveys consistently showing a strong majority in favor of "land for peace" and reconciled to contiguous Palestinian statehood throughout those years, would emphatically argue that a genuine and profound shift had in fact taken place in their country's cultural disposition, marked by greater sympathy for the diplomatic argument over the military-security one.

This author's own reading of the Camp David II proceedings finds the argument of positive convergence the most convincing—at least at the level of the day-to-day peace processors. This explanation, however, only renders more acute the question of why the U.S. initiative failed if, in fact, the practical negotiators had really been seeking the middle ground of understanding. Let me offer two reasons for the failure, the first being a tendency to impart too much importance to intercultural bridging. Apropos of President Clinton's above-cited praise for the Regulars, peace professors and peace processors on the eve of the summit united in gambling "that by the time we got to the end of the road, there would be enough knowledge and trust and understanding of each other's positions that these huge, epochal issues could be resolved."[49] The truth is that cross-cultural understanding can take you quite far—but only so far, and usually not far enough.

This is because—and here we move to the second reason—all of the advice in the world on how to make social and psychological inroads is of little avail unless preached and practiced by those at the very top. The finest manuals on cultural learning cannot override the will and the political mandate of leaders who possess the final say on negotiation strategy, tactics, and policy, but who, like Arafat, prove either unbending or ultimately unwilling to commit; or, like Israeli civilian leaders, are surrounded by professional military security specialists advocating the strictest construction of security, as well as being dependent upon their endorsement and support; or, as in the case of Ehud Barak, are themselves ultimately still wedded to the security subculture mindset. As Bill Clinton, the convenor of Camp David II, himself ruefully concluded, "Nothing is agreed until everything is agreed."[50]

In the end, the search for causal explanations must look beyond culture. No matter how conciliatory Israeli delegates may have seen themselves, and whatever the extent of greater cultural sophistication by 2000 among ordinary Israelis and Palestinians, and particularly among the Regulars, conciliation and cultural sophistication did not manifest themselves in the Summiteers. Camp David II peacemaking floundered because all of the suppressed main substantive issues on the agenda—from sovereignty to the plight of the Arab refugees and Jerusalem—known since 1993 yet artfully papered over during the post-Oslo era by ambiguity, finally, and belatedly, surfaced in all their explosiveness.

Permanent-status talks exposed not only the complexity of these divisive issues but also just how divided the two sides really were, and are, over them. No cultural sensitivity in and of itself could possibly compensate for the paralytic effect of two sets of vital interests incompatible with each other, especially once the negotiations exposed the true extent of Palestinian intransigence. Put differently, no mathematical equations could satisfactorily solve the deepest complexities of reapportioning territory, segmenting Jerusalem, alleviating security dilemmas, and escorting home-coming Palestinian refugees from Lebanon and Jordan to an agreed-upon safe haven that would not prejudice Israel's pre-standing right to exist.

Consequently, when interests and personality came to the fore in a strained diplomatic atmosphere, many of the positive cultural symmetries unraveled quickly, thus bearing out Janice Stein's point about "the per-sistence of enemy images."[51] Accordingly, old and familiar prejudices, fears, suspicions, and insecurities resurfaced during the summit itself, and became yet more pronounced in the violent aftermath to Camp David II, sweeping aside the logic of peaceful conflict resolution in Filastin/ Eretz Yisrael.

There is no disputing that in July 2000 Israeli policy was Prime Minister Barak's policy as much as Palestinian decisions were Chairman Arafat's decisions. To an extraordinary extent, the assertiveness and centralist leadership command style of both, their subjective situational reassess-ments, unpredictable mood swings, and odd personal behavior in general ensured that Camp David II would join history's list of Middle East missed opportunities.

Of Arafat, the sullen prisoner of Camp David, much has been written. In particular, commentators note his open lack of enthusiasm in the planning stage regarding the summit's bad timing and insufficient preparations, his isolation and deepening sense of being pressured by sinister Israeli-U.S. collusion, and his refusal to accept what were in his eyes insulting terms offered by Israel that did not go far enough in fulfilling Palestinian aspi-rations but yet endangered his own personal standing in the Arab and Muslim worlds.[52] Israeli portraits of Arafat are less charitable, fed by firsthand reports from members of the Israeli delegation, promoted most ardently by Barak himself in his controversial *New York Review of Books* interview,[53] and endorsed by Dennis Ross on the American side.[54] These sketches present him as singularly uncooperative and mean-spirited, either unwilling or unable to rise to the historic occasion.

Arafat being Arafat, his negotiating posture at least had the benefit of consistency and might have been predicted by Israeli analysts as they pre-pared in 2000 for the fateful summit. With due respect to Chairman Arafat, and to President Clinton, more intriguing is the question of Prime Minister Barak's personal contribution to the outcome in his capacity as Israel's head of delegation, principal bargaining representative, and foremost negotiation culture bearer.

The Character-Culture Nexus

For paradigmatic purposes, Ehud Barak mirrors an entire *problematique* as yet undeveloped in the scientific literature on intercultural negotiation. The notion of negotiating across cultures—what Richard Solomon terms the "binary process"[55]—still refers exclusively to two nations or two state actors. There is good reason, however, why cross-cultural analysis should be extended to apply equally to contending *sub*cultures—the diplomatic and the security—*within* a single national culture, *inside* a single state actor, and, indeed, successfully or unsuccessfully *internalized* by a solitary national leader.

After all, national cultures are not a seamless cloth but a finely woven fabric, carefully selected, patterned, and customized by master tailors, in this instance, political leaders. Diplomatic negotiation is one of those points where abstract state interests and national cultures are entrusted into the hands of the individual statesman, who then interprets, rethreads, and refashions according to his or her character, policy designs, and negotiating style.

The scientific study of nations and their negotiating cultures must therefore integrate the individual level of analysis, acknowledging the influence of personality and leadership psychology on whether countries incline more toward redesigning traditional cultural patterns or toward preserving them.[56] This spotlight on leaders and on negotiator preferences is especially warranted in the instance of Israel, where the imprint of personality on policy is so profound and where a distinguished defense career is still the best political entrance ticket for "parachuting" into high public office. A leader-oriented focus also serves as a healthy antidote to the overdose of attention given to ideational and institutional considerations by constructivists at the expense of personality and personalities in Israeli policy.[57]

Arguably, no Israeli leader better illustrates the importance to negotiation of an individual's personality and psychology than Barak. Chosen for closer study here, his summit behavior and negotiating culture bring to light discrepancies of two different types: an inconsistency with accepted Israeli negotiating practices and bargaining patterns, and contradictions within the logic of Barak's own peace strategy. Moreover, Barak's further contribution lies in provoking a number of ideas pertinent to the comparative analysis of negotiation and culture. In his negotiations at Camp David, he did not so much personify the flaws of the security subculture as exemplify (a) just how powerful and pervasive an unadulterated security subculture can be; (b) how easy it is when negotiating conflict to succumb to the logic of its reasoning; and (c) just how difficult it is for all parties interested in resolving international conflicts either to *integrate* the two subcultures of security and diplomacy or, alternatively, to *traverse* from one orientation to the other.

Building Mistrust

Surprising perhaps to outsiders, the consensus Israeli view of Ehud Barak is singularly unflattering. Henry Kissinger may wish to regard him as "the most daring and by far the most conciliatory Israeli prime minister in history";[58] and President Clinton might have chosen to single him out for showing "particular courage, vision and an understanding of the historical importance of this moment."[59] However, Aluf Benn, respected diplomatic correspondent for the Israeli daily newspaper *Haaretz,* pronounces Barak's "all-or-nothing" approach "brave but flawed."[60] In a circulated paper titled "From Oslo to Taba: What Went Wrong?" Ron Pundak, one of the first Israelis to meet with the Palestinians in 1993, charges that Barak's negotiating technique was stained "by arrogance, single-mindedness and the fallacy that 'only I have the big picture, and only I know and understand it all.'"[61]

In this critical vein, Reuven Merhav, a former director-general of the Foreign Ministry airlifted to Camp David on short notice by the prime minister to advise on Jerusalem in the very midst of the heated deliberations, adds another note of implied censure by dryly commenting that "in no other question was the unique lack, or belatedness of the preparations of the government of Israel so marked as in the question of Jerusalem."[62] Nor can any reader of the two detailed insider accounts of events from 1999 to 2001 by Gilead Sher and Shlomo Ben-Ami help but take due notice of the couched criticisms of their boss's conduct, and in particular of Barak's reluctance to accept advice on dispelling rather than sowing Palestinian distrust.

It is true that, given the substance of the dispute and its track record of intractability, nothing might have saved the 2000 summit from failure. It was for the most part an ill-advised, ill-timed attempt to induce ripeness. Nevertheless, criticism from so many nonideological and nonpartisan quarters in Israel suggests more than a little discomfort at Barak's personal handling of the negotiations and personal performance, with closed-mindedness, condescension, and unpreparedness forming merely part of the indictment. The weight of mounting firsthand evidence confirms that his tough stand of "take it or leave it" toward Arafat runs counter to the essence of the diplomatic culture that, at the other polar extreme, in principle pronounces everything negotiable. Only serving to compound his, and Israel's, problem in projecting negotiating credibility was the mounting discrepancy between this inflexible declaratory posture, on the one hand, and, on the other, his sanctioning even as late as Taba of nonstop reformulations—consistently downward—of the Israeli position on Jerusalem as well as on every one of the agenda items. In short, Prime Minister Barak may have talked all-or-nothing but he practiced compromise and concession in what can only be regarded as one of the worst fusions imaginable of the military and diplomatic subcultures.

In fairness, and as evidenced in every one of the retrospective Camp David II narratives—Israeli, Palestinian, and American—future historians and students of conflict resolution will pronounce both Arafat and Barak misfits, suited neither to each other nor for peacemaking. The eve of the summit found Arafat sullen and recalcitrant, Barak transparent in his overeagerness for closure. The following days saw the two men moving in opposite directions, Barak losing confidence in his strategy, while the Palestinian leader became increasingly resolute and unbending. The more Barak pressed for a straightforward bilateral accord in keeping with the very essence of Oslo, the deeper became Arafat's idée fixe about the essential need for a central international role and outside presence.

Although success clearly depended upon Barak gaining Arafat's consent, the prime minister did not really make a concerted effort to gain the Palestinian Authority chief's respect or confidence, let alone to build close rapport. Given the prime minister's long military career of studying the enemy, surely he must have natively understood Raymond Cohen's basic cultural distinction between "problem-oriented" and "relationship-oriented" modes.[64] Evidently he did not, for he proceeded to concentrate exclusively on the business at hand while neglecting the personal side of negotiation. As the talks lengthened, the lack of trust grew and personal suspicion deepened, with each man questioning the other's motives and doubting his sincerity. In such a poisoned atmosphere, the two men played out a sequence of moves and countermoves until, finally, Arafat's resistance won out over Barak's insistence.

Each of the two Summiteers displayed variant forms of truculent behavior. Alone together, and deliberately confrontational, they persisted in talking past each other, which worked against American cultural negotiation proclivities, upset the U.S. strategy (also Israel's), and devastated Clinton in his role as convenor, host, and presumed honest broker. Consistent with the traditional American approach, the president relied on two favored techniques, the first being bonhomie, and the second what Raymond Cohen labels "concession-convergence"[65] and William Zartman calls "the 50% solution."[66] In two words: congeniality and compromise.

However, as evidenced from their body language and reciprocal boycott, attempts to create a positive and favorable atmosphere proved embarrassingly ineffective. Neither Arafat nor Barak came to Camp David enjoying a reputation for conviviality or had a penchant for small talk. Besides, from the very first day the former signaled he was not in a cheerful mood, while the latter's sole interest lay in getting down to brass tacks and systematically attacking each of the agenda items.[67] Similarly, while Clinton and his team intuitively worked from the premise that negotiating parties will typically start out from different positions but then arrive at a middle ground through tit-for-tat concessions, the two leading Middle East participants insisted upon playing by a different set of rules.

Ehud Barak compounded his own plight by being of two minds. Both Shimon Peres and Yitzhak Rabin, once having made their strategic decision to commit fully to the Oslo spirit of good-faith negotiation, came perhaps as close as possible to making the wrenching kind of psychocultural transition peacemaking requires. At least publicly, each man expressed few misgivings and showed no signs of wavering from the Oslo commitment. Each of them, albeit with different degrees of enthusiasm and with different personal styles, adapted to a more positive, less ambivalent image of the Palestinians, their relationship with Israel, and their role in the negotiation process. In other words, Peres and Rabin were at one with themselves.

Not so Barak. The rules he used in bargaining with the Palestinians represent an uneasy amalgam of the two contending Israeli diplomatic and security subcultures. Throughout his stint as prime minister from 1999 to 2001, he comes across as constantly torn between the subcultures of coercion and persuasion and their corresponding images of the Palestinian-as-enemy and the Palestinian-as-partner. Unable to resolve his own dilemma in trying to splice key strands in the military ethos with the prospective fruits of peace, he found himself stuck in the interstices between the security and the political-diplomatic subcultures. Barak's personal ambivalence could not help but insinuate itself into Israel's official bargaining stance. In short, as a peace strategist and direct negotiator, he was successful neither at escaping his past nor in imposing his iron will on the Israeli-Palestinian present.

In the diplomatic mode, he did acknowledge the Palestinians as Israel's only directly concerned party and did adopt his Labor Alignment party's slogan of "land for peace" and the party's platform of maximum separation between the two peoples. He committed himself to pursuing the diplomatic negotiation track and, as shown at Camp David, had prepared himself mentally and politically for what he thought were the necessary concessions Israel would have to make. Lastly, he identified with the imperative for reaching an immediate, comprehensive, and definitive resolution of the Palestine conflict.

Not to be taken lightly, these adjustments meant breaking with what Abba Eban described in specific reference to Yitzhak Shamir as "a passionate love affair with the status quo,"[68] but which applied just as well to each of Barak's predecessors since 1967. In fact, the more Barak deviated from those Arab-Israeli negotiating conventions that center around feigning, reconnoitering, attrition tactics, opaqueness, and playing for time, and the more he presented himself, instead, as forceful, explicit, urgent, and result oriented, the closer Barak came to resembling Americans in their distinctive and pragmatic negotiating style.[69] He did so at the expense of losing credibility with the Palestinian delegation as a whole, whose members had difficulty reading Barak and knowing exactly what game he was playing, while further distancing himself from Arafat, who had his suspicions to begin with.

The problem is that Barak the general-turned-statesman sought to negotiate his adroit diplomatic strategy while still conditioned to a career-long professional military mindset. Supporting the proposition that occupational background and training are a key influence upon negotiating style,[70] Barak in the end remained a product of the IDF mentality and of the security establishment's negotiation subculture. The fact that his idiosyncratic personality and character traits dovetailed with the institutional culture, thereby sharpening rather than smoothing possible rough edges, certainly did not help him in his role as peace negotiator.

Ralph White, aiming to illustrate how commonplace misperception is, lists six distinctive forms: diabolical enemy-image; virile self-image; moral self-image; selective inattention; absence of empathy; and military over-confidence.[71] During Camp David II, Barak seems to have exhibited most, if not all, of these forms. Whether he did so intentionally or not is beside the point because in the end this is how he was perceived, and by the very people in the Palestinian camp whose confidence and cooperation became critical for the success of the entire endeavor. There was, for instance, Barak's military demeanor, the swagger of a decorated field commander confident of his own judgment and of his ability to take charge of any situation. Accustomed to issuing military orders and making major command decisions, as civilian prime minister and head of delegation he insisted upon concentrating all authority in himself, effectively precluding the kind of teamwork and interaction Menachem Begin encouraged at Camp David in 1978, and that served Israeli interests well at the time.

Then there is his puzzling attitude toward the Palestinian side. Charles Enderlin, in chronicling Barak's repeated snubbing of Arafat, relates, for example, Barak's refusal to accept his own advisers' suggestions that he speak directly with Arafat at any of several critical moments; how at a meal lasting two hours on Sunday, July 17, not once did he turn his head toward the PLO chairman seated next to him; and how, upon entering the dining room on Thursday, July 21, he turned away without acknowledging Arafat.[72] Agha and Malley, with Hanieh to corroborate, fault Barak more generally for his tactical clumsiness, lack of personal touch, and inability to create working relationships—all of which the Palestinians interpreted not as distress signals but as signs of arrogance and disrespect.[73]

Yet of all the possible negotiating culture missteps, arguably the most telling is the military overconfidence Ehud Barak brought to bear. One fatal manifestation was his attempt to convert a pillar of IDF strategy — seizing the initiative from one's opponent by moving to the offense, concentrating upon a single objective, amassing forces, applying pressure, boxing the enemy into a corner, and then taking his targeted positions by storm—into a bold diplomatic bargaining strategy. Besides imposing a time limitation of his own on reaching a final-status agreement with the Palestinians, he presented each of a succession of Israeli packaged proposals and conditions as a take-it-or-leave-it offer. Agha and Malley complete the picture for us by explaining how the dynamic played out so badly. "By presenting early positions as bottom lines, the Israelis provoked the Palestinians' mistrust; by subsequently shifting them, they whetted the Palestinians' appetite."[74] That appetite only increased when Arafat and his advisers came to read Barak as an Israeli prime minister floundering in light of his boastful pledges and eroding political standing at home, and thus increasingly desperate for success.

As a form of applying pressure, the Barak summit game plan backfired badly, principally for the reason that international negotiation differs fundamentally from theoretical military science. Unlike military sieges, pitched battles, or, for that matter, domestic political contests, at the diplomatic bargaining table, one's opponent may not be so easily drawn in or obliged to go along. In any event, Arafat withstood Barak's (and Clinton's) pressure and did not yield his own deeply entrenched defensive position. Recalling how at the later Taba talks the Barak government improved its territorial bid by offering to cede 97 percent of the West Bank to Palestinian control, Abu Ala, who headed the Palestinian delegation, refused even that late proposal and at Arafat's express instruction held to the opening demand for "the entire 100 percent, and not one centimeter less."[75]

Conclusions

From the larger standpoint of culture and its role in negotiating conflict, this chapter advises looking more closely for indications of cultural heterogeneity and pluralism even within any single given national culture. Such diversities will usually find expression through alternative and typically competing subcultures—in the instance of Israel, the security- and the diplomacy-oriented subcultures. Whether treated as comprehensive worldviews, religious and ideological mindsets, organizational subcultures, or different orientations toward political and international problems, in matters of *mediniyut chutz u'bitachon* (foreign and security policy), the Israeli military establishment and intelligence community traditionally gave, and instinctively still give, far greater consideration and decisive weight to the national security concept—and in its most physical, individual, and immediate sense—than to the more sophisticated and seemingly more distant foreign affairs component. As shown here, in the same way that this calculus impacts on every other aspect of Israeli life in the continuing felt absence of peace, normalcy, and reasonably assured security, so does it dominate Israeli attitudes and approaches to negotiation with all Arab parties, and with Palestinians in particular.

This said, it is nonetheless evident that a fundamental rethinking of Israel's national political culture and of the proper relationship between diplomacy and security had begun before the Oslo opening and was intensified immediately thereafter, a rethinking in favor of permitting diplomacy and negotiating statecraft to take the lead in crafting Israeli Middle Eastern policy and relations. But then the derailment of the Oslo process effectively halted this closer integration of the diplomatic subculture into the national ethos and into governmental policymaking procedures.

Premier Barak's own personal defeat because of the misapplication of lessons and tactics learned on the battlefield to the bargaining table dramatically illustrates this larger national setback for hopes of smooth, linear cultural change. If his intention was to effect a sweeping change in the language and culture of Israeli-Palestinian relations, then his plans tragically miscarried. His efforts to straddle both the diplomacy-oriented and the security-oriented subcultures certainly did not achieve the definitive peace breakthrough he sought. If he meant only to reveal "the real Arafat" and the true nature of nonnegotiable Palestinian demands, then this exposé might have been engineered differently, should have been forced much closer to 1993 than to 2000 by any of his three immediate predecessors, Rabin, Peres, or Netanyahu, and has come at a grievous human cost for both sides. Poorly executed at Camp David II and discredited by Taba,[76] the Barak approach of "hard softness" or "soft hardness" was then promptly jettisoned. In the face of the dismal outcome of negotiations over permanent status and escalating Palestinian armed resistance, Ariel

Sharon, Barak's successor, unabashedly reverted to playing negotiation by more stringent Middle Eastern and Israeli security rules, variously interpreted, depending upon one's degree of cynicism, or realism, as: might makes right; no negotiation; unconditional surrender; there are no rules; security rules.

Two sets of conclusions are thus warranted. One set is of more specific relevance for understanding how disillusioning the Camp David denouement to Oslo has been for many Israelis who, with ample provocation from Palestinian militants, have gone from negating to negotiating and now back to negating. The other set consists of theoretical observations in the context of negative intercultural reinforcement.

Regarding the first set of conclusions, as a group Israeli participants close to the Oslo process found endgame Palestinian behavior at Camp David altogether objectionable. Interestingly, those most appalled were prominent national figures aligned with the dovish "Peace Now" camp such as the author Amos Oz and Laborite politicians such as Yossi Sarid and Shlomo Ben-Ami, who until then had been outspoken enthusiasts for a far-reaching reconciliation between Jewish and Arab nationalism along the visionary lines of the book *The New Middle East,* authored by Shimon Peres in the early, euphoric aftermath of Oslo.[77]

Particularly disconcerting in Israeli eyes were:

- The Palestinians' insistence upon sole victimization and its corollary, full entitlement. Seeing themselves as the only aggrieved party, they offered not a trace of contrition but rather demanded absolute compensation for the historic wrongs claimed to have been committed against them by Zionism. This was hardly a position or an attitude conducive to the give-and-take of negotiation.

- The Palestinians' refusal to endorse Israeli compromise formulas or to offer formal counterproposals on the grounds that they had already recognized Israel and had agreed to limit Arab territorial demands to only 22 percent of British-mandated Palestine, and that further concessions were impossible.

- Palestinian intolerance for fundamental Israeli rights and claims, despite Israel having agreed, for example, to negotiate under the principle of parity by conceding a full measure of equivalence in size and quantity in any prospective land exchange, or "swap."

- Arafat's perceived disdain for Israel's most basic insecurities and values, as demonstrated in his insistence on the right of return of Palestinian refugees to Israel proper, and his off-handed dismissal of all Jewish religious and historical roots in the Temple Mount in Jerusalem—tantamount to delegitimizing not only Zionist and Israeli credentials but the very authenticity of Judaism.

Seen in Israeli eyes as a flagrant provocation, and coming so very near the end of the Camp David negotiating round, this latter expression of rejectionism in particular left even the most open-minded delegation members incredulous.

The felt absence of Palestinian remorse, compromise, or empathy was upsetting enough to Israeli peace processors. Worse yet, Arafat's unbending negativism, no longer tolerable as simply a bargaining ploy, and dictated to all members of his delegation, also represented unacceptable backsliding from earlier concessions and joint understandings. As one major example, at the very time and place when bold leadership in command decisions was called for, Arafat's appeals at Camp David for Arab and Islamic support—in effect conferring Arab and Islamic veto power on any future arrangement for Jerusalem—were read in Israeli circles as a conscious Palestinian reversion to external dependency after the PLO leader's historic 1993 Oslo declaration of independence from Arab world rulers.[78] Israeli strategists were therefore left no choice but to conclude that Arafat fully intended to halt the peace process well short of finality.

In the final paragraph of his Palestinian narrative on the events at the Camp David summit, Akram Hanieh supplies the following parting vignette: "As they looked back at the retreat from the windows of their cars, the Palestinian negotiators heaved a deep sigh of relief. They had stated a clear No to the United States on U.S. territory. There was no bravado. It was a No that was politically, nationally, and historically correct and necessary to put the peace process on the right track."[79] Whether it was correct and necessary or not, Israeli proponents of direct peacemaking could only wonder at the choice of priorities: the United States before Israel; and addiction to yesterday and past grievances over making tomorrow's history and improving tomorrow's prospects. Here, perhaps, is the essence of the gap separating Israeli and Palestinian negotiating cultures at the moment when the bridging processes launched with such fanfare in 1993 ended so abruptly in 2000–2001, giving way to the darker forces of intolerance and ill will.

Nearly two years later, in charging Arafat with mendacity, Ehud Barak, by then former prime minister, inexcusably fell back upon negative cultural stereotyping when he commented of the Palestinians in general, "They are products of a culture in which to tell a lie . . . creates no dissonance. They don't suffer from the problem of telling lies that exists in Judeo-Christian culture. Truth is seen as an irrelevant category. There is only that which serves your purpose and that which doesn't. They see themselves as emissaries of a national movement for whom everything is permissible. There is no such thing as 'the truth.'"[80] What might possibly account for such cultural atavism? The ignominy of embarrassing personal and political failure? Legitimate concern at telltale signs of either conflict under-ripeness or over-ripeness? Perhaps the deep chasm reopened after a full decade of cultural bridging and striving for cultural fluency? Or a lifetime of internalizing the security subculture? I do not believe that any single explanation suffices. Nevertheless, Barak's outburst does lead directly to a final observation about culture-based studies of peacemaking and cross-cultural communication processes.

A survey of the literature indicates a strong normative bias in the attention shown almost exclusively to positive political learning. Joseph Ginat, for instance, comments that "in negotiations the parties come to know the basic cultural norms and customs of the other side. This familiarity helps to break down barriers to sincere discussion, compromise, and accord."[81] Similarly, in her important essay on intergroup differences, does Janice Stein define learning as "*changes* in images and identity that *promote* conflict *routinization, reduction,* and *resolution.*"[82] Note the implicit assumption that diplomatic learning exercises such as negotiation and bargaining and problem solving are linear, that somehow such processes can only improve adversarial relationships while fostering understandings and building trust.

To be sure, interactions do develop, contexts do evolve, images are altered, and significant changes do take place over the trajectory of a conflict and in the natural course of getting to, sitting at, and getting up from the negotiating table. However, we should always be prepared for reverses and anticipate a possible deterioration in relations if and when a given dialogue exposes rather than erases sharp differences. Familiarity through negotiation encounters is as liable to engender contempt as empathy or respect. Bargaining positions may either soften or harden as a result of adversaries meeting and talking to each other. Two sides are as likely to recoil *from* each other as they are to link up *with* each other halfway, shake hands, and embrace. Tolerance is balanced by intolerance, respect by disrespect, understanding by misunderstanding, trust by distrust and mistrust, collaboration by discord, reconciliation by irreconcilability, and the healing effects of culture by the distorting effects of culture.

In sum, realism mandates acknowledging that just as images can change positively, improving incrementally over time, so, unfortunately, can they change negatively, deteriorating either abruptly or by smaller increments. The latter is often the case, especially once ambiguity and goodwill wear off, revealing the core substantive divide over tangible or affective interests. Reverses are also often associated with the intrusion into negotiations of dominant personalities, whose impact is to negate whatever broader intercultural bridge building may have accomplished up to that point.

Herein lie but a few of the sobering lessons imparted by Israel's lengthening Sisyphean experience in spanning the manmade Israeli-Palestinian, Arab-Jewish cultural divide. That both longer-term history and the annals of recent years are branded Sisyphean should not be read to imply that of necessity all further efforts at bridging the divide are inevitably doomed. Such fatalism is misplaced, but what the record does suggest is that Israelis, and Palestinians, need to work hard at learning to understand the other side's language, history, value systems, and culture, and that, no less crucially, they must still learn to reshape their own respective negotiating cultures. In the instance of Israel, this will require a renewed conscious and sustained effort at modifying an unalloyed security outlook. Two keystones of all such present and future efforts will be the incorporation of key elements of the subculture of diplomacy, accompanied and abetted by positive reinforcement from Arab leaders and Palestinian society that the higher road of diplomacy and risk taking are indeed warranted on Israel's part.

In concluding, let there be no room for misunderstanding: true peace, like cultural change and the negotiation process itself, cannot, indeed dare not, be unilateral. Israel is neither engaged in making peace nor in negotiating with itself. Just as I imagine Palestinian moderation is dependent upon and awaits gestures and moves by Israel, so, too, are the Israeli diplomatic subculture's prospects for seeing security in coexistence enhanced by signals, signs, and then public acts by the emerging generation of Arafat's successors in jointly persisting at the task of formulating workable, livable solutions to the core substantive issues of mutual security, Palestinian viability, refugee rehabilitation, and, of course, Jerusalem's governance and special status. If the long Arab-Jewish struggle teaches anything, it is that with cultural understanding and sensitivity everything becomes possible; without them, nothing is possible.

From an Israeli perspective, the fuller import is unmistakable. Aside from the grievous cost in human lives, surely the most lamentable consequence of the breakdown of the Oslo process is the depletion of former reserves of trust that Israelis were prepared to invest in diplomatic discourse and in nurturing peace through direct good-faith negotiation around the bargaining table. This trust they are no longer inclined to bestow so readily, either to the existing Palestinian leadership or even to mediated negotiating processes.

Still, whatever else it may offer, the singularly eventful Oslo decade furnishes the precedent, the logic, and the potential for a far-reaching Israeli-Palestinian strategic option, one that proposes substituting opportunity for hurting stalemate, functional cooperation for self-help, mutuality for unilateralism, benefits for costs, and win-win for zero-sum. Exercising this option, however, will in all likelihood require the parties to lower their expectations from achieving peace with full reconciliation to accepting, at least initially, some form of wary coexistence, or "soft" partition—a type of forced coexistence and cultural tolerance that derives from the existential need to cohabit in this uncompromising land.

Notes

More than the usual obligatory acknowledgment or word of appreciation, the author expresses genuine admiration to the following people for their extensive comments, good counsel, detailed criticisms, and timely correctives in reading several chapter drafts: Professor Avi Ben-Zvi, Moti Cristal, Adrian Klieman, Professor Yoram Peri, Dr. Howard Rosen, Dr. Tamara Wittes, three outside commentators, and, not least but editorially last, Nigel Quinney.

1. See, for example, Aharon Cohen, *Israel and the Arab World* (London: W. H. Allen, 1970).

2. Israelis regard with equal astonishment and incomprehension statements —which clash so glaringly with the biblical injunction "And thou shall choose

life"—like that by Abdul Aziz Rantisi, a top Hamas official: "We love martyrdom and we seek martyrdom," in praising a fallen militant leader as one of "the men of the dark night." Quoted by Amos Harel, Jonathan Lis, and Yair Ettinger, "Thousands Flock to Hamas Leader's Funeral," *Haaretz,* August 24, 2003.

3. David K. Shipler, for example, writes that Jerusalem represents "a center of conflicting absolutes, of certainty, of righteousness" for both peoples. *Arab and Jew* (New York: Penguin Books, 1986), 7. He also notes, "Both peoples are victims. Each has suffered at the hands of outsiders, and each has been wounded by the other" (8). Tamara Wittes, in her dissertation, "Symbols and Security in Ethnic Conflict," and discussion of Israeli and Palestinian "core identity needs and aspirations" and "core themes," similarly points out how Zionists and Palestinians both share a preoccupation with certain key "communal markers": land possession, the right of return to self-defined homelands, perceived insecurity, victimization, and the quest for legitimacy (PhD diss., Georgetown University, 2000), 77. To Shipler's and Wittes's inventory of common denominators, I would add negotiating by Middle East rules of conduct.

4. Jane Corbin, *Gaza First: The Secret Norway Channel to Peace between Israel and the PLO* (London: Bloomsbury, 1994), 213.

5. "Proximate policymakers" refers to those not directly charged with deciding policy yet whose status and input indirectly contribute to shaping the policy decision, to framing options, and to shaping the policy debate. See Aharon Klieman, "Proximate Policy-Makers," in *Global Politics: Essays in Honour of David Vital,* ed. Abraham Ben-Zvi and Aharon Klieman (London: Frank Cass, 2001), 99–117.

6. Henry A. Kissinger, "Domestic Structure and Foreign Policy," in *International Politics and Foreign Policy,* ed. James N. Rosenau (New York: Free Press, 1969), 266.

7. Evidenced by an entire body of literature—theoretical, case specific, and comparative—recent years find a marked upsurge of research into culture's importance in foreign policy decision making and for international communication processes. Once downplayed, culture's explanatory power is respected today, with many studies and country monographs offering it as the determinant variable shaping respective negotiating stances.

8. The logic behind this notion of an emerging international culture, including common diplomatic and negotiation cultures, fueled by globalization, is reflected, for instance, in *International Negotiation: A Cross-Cultural Perspective,* by Glen Fisher (Chicago: Intercultural Press, 1980). Fisher sensed already then that "the modern intensity of international interaction . . . has produced something of an internationalized 'culture' which reduces the clash of cultural background and stereotyped images." Fisher attributes the emergence of "international conventions of negotiation" in particular to U.S. cultural dominance in light of the fact that "many otherwise 'foreign' counterparts are accommodating to the American style of negotiation," with one of the guiding American assumptions being that there are no insurmountable differences that cannot be overcome with dialogue (17, 8).

Samuel P. Huntington offers a different interpretation in his highly debated article "The Clash of Civilizations?" *Foreign Affairs* 72, no. 3 (Summer 1993): 22–49, and in an expanded book version (question mark deleted), *The Clash of Civilizations and the Remaking of World Order* (New York: Simon & Schuster, 1996). In both works he argues the greater prospect of a world of civilizations—multipolar and multicivilizational—than of a universal world civilization. Also taking issue are Jean M. Hiltrop and Sheila Udall, *The Essence of Negotiation* (Englewood Cliffs, NJ: Prentice Hall, 1995). See chapter 5, "Negotiating among Cultures," where they warn of the mistake in ignoring differences between national cultures when discussing negotiation processes.

9. The discussion in this section is influenced by the pioneering work of Elizabeth Kier on "organizational culture" and the important distinctions she introduces. See Elizabeth Kier, "Culture and French Military Doctrine before World War II," in *The Culture of National Security: Norms and Identity in World Politics,* ed. Peter J. Katzenstein (New York: Columbia University Press, 1996), 186–215; together with the notion of "political-military culture" as used and developed by Thomas U. Berger, in his chapter in the same volume, "Norms, Identity, and National Security in Germany and Japan," 317–356.

Defining "organizational culture" as "the set of basic assumptions, values, norms, beliefs, and formal knowledge that shapes collective understandings," Kier goes on to demonstrate how the culture of an organization "shapes its members' perceptions and affects what they notice and how they interpret it; it screens out some parts of 'reality' while magnifying others" (202). Accepting the presence of several such "subcultures," she then addresses the military's "organizational culture" and "the interests that military organizations bring to doctrinal decisions" (203) and also notes how "few institutions devote as many resources to the assimilation of their members as does the military" (202).

10. On political culture in Israel, see Yossi Beilin, *Israel: A Concise Political History* (New York: St. Martin's Press, 1992), chap. 6.

11. One of the more recent and original efforts at characterizing rival schools of thought is Jonathan Rynhold's recasting of the Israeli left into two subcultures: "Realist"-Statist and "Liberal" Progressive, with Ehud Barak, like most of his former career military colleagues, gravitating toward the former and its postulates of the need for disengagement from the Palestinians, treating Oslo as a test

of Arab intentions, cementing ties to the United States, and seeing the peace process as linked to domestic morale. "Making Sense of Tragedy: Barak, the Israeli Left and the Oslo Peace Process," *Israel Studies Forum* 19, no. 1 (Fall 2003): 9–33.

12. One of the few serious inquiries into the security culture referred to here, to success in creating a broad "security consensus," and to dominance by the security sector has been accomplished by Reuven Pedatzur in his chapter "Ben-Gurion's Enduring Legacy" in *Security Concerns: Insights from the Israeli Experience,* ed. Daniel Bar-Tal, Dan Jacobson, and Aharon Klieman (Greenwich, CT: JAI Press, 1998), 139–164.

13. "Nothing Left but the Reflex," *Haaretz,* June 20, 2003.

14. "An Abiding Faith in Force," *Haaretz,* October 9, 2003. Pointing out the terrible collateral damage on thought processes in Israel inflicted by the upsurge in Middle East violence since 2000, Benn observes that because Israel "is back to its old belief that military force will defeat the Arabs," in deliberations under the Sharon government, "non-violent solutions are not even raised, let alone discussed."

15. Other scholars, like Alastair Iain Johnston, prefer the term "strategic culture." In his study of Chinese strategic culture, *Cultural Realism* (Princeton, NJ: Princeton University Press, 1995), he defines "strategic culture" as "an integrated system of symbols that acts to establish pervasive and long-lasting grand strategic preferences by formulating concepts of the role and efficacy of military force in interstate political affairs, and by clothing these conceptions with such an aura of factuality that the strategic preferences seem uniquely realistic and efficacious" (36).

16. Compare Gil Merom, "Israel's National Security and the Myth of Exceptionalism," *Political Science Quarterly* 114, no. 3 (1999): 409–434, with Yechezkel Dror, "On the Uniqueness of Israel: Multiple Readings," in *Israel in Comparative Perspective*, ed. Michael N. Barnett (Albany, NY: State University of New York Press, 1996), 245–257 (chap. 10).

17. A useful compendium of essays looking at national security's primacy and its multiple implications for the country's national psyche, politics, and social life is Bar-Tal, Jacobson, and Klieman, eds., *Security Concerns.*

18. According to a 2003 World Terrorism Index released by the World Markets Research Center, as a terror risk, Israel ranks second only to Colombia as a target country, followed by Pakistan, the United States, the Philippines, and Indonesia. Don Van Natta, Jr., "U.S. No. 4 as a Target of Terror," *International Herald Tribune,* August 18, 2003.

19. Beilin, *Israel: A Concise Political History,* 154 (italics mine).

20. The best single treatment of the civil-military relationship is still Yoram Peri, *Between Battles and Ballots: The Israeli Military in Politics* (Cambridge: Cambridge University Press, 1983).

21. Uzi Benziman, "When the Army Takes Off Its Uniform," *Haaretz,* December 7, 2003.

22. Aharon Klieman, "Israel: Succumbing to Foreign Ministry Declinism," in *Foreign Ministries: Change and Adaptation,* ed. Brian Hocking (London: Macmillan, 1999), 75–101 (chap. 5).

23. See Yoram Peri, *The Israeli Military and Israel's Palestinian Policy,* Peaceworks no. 47 (Washington, DC: United States Institute of Peace, 2002).

24. Carl von Clausewitz, *On War,* ed. and trans. Michael Howard and Peter Paret (New York and Toronto: Alfred A. Knopf, 1993), 731.

25. In his paper on joint Israeli-Palestinian security cooperation from 1993 until 2000, Lieutenant Colonel (res.) Kobi Michael, who had directed the IDF apparatus for coordinating security enforcement in the West Bank, describes attitudes on the Israeli side lacking in trust and riddled with "patronization and condescension" in the face of nepotism, organized corruption, and incompetence on the Palestinian side. Amos Harel, "Why Security Cooperation after Oslo Never Worked," *Haaretz,* August 17, 2003, 2.

26. Bruce Riedel, a Clinton adviser for Middle East affairs, reports an Israel initiative at the time of Camp David calling for a U.S.-Israel mutual defense treaty that would have constituted a transformation of the Israeli-American security partnership. Interestingly, the draft agreement was presented by two of Premier Ehud Barak's closest confidants, Danny Yatom and Zvi Stauber, both of them former army career officers. However, because President Clinton triangulated the deal, making it conditional on Israel finalizing its own agreement with the Palestinians, nothing ever came of the initiative. "Barak-Clinton Camp David Defense Deal Revealed," *Jerusalem Post,* July 16, 2002 (http://www.jpost.com/servl).

27. Eliot A. Cohen, *Supreme Command: Soldiers, Statesmen, and Leadership in Wartime* (New York: Free Press, 2002), 11–12.

28. Peri, *The Israeli Military and Israel's Palestinian Policy,* 23–25.

29. Shlomo Ben-Ami, *Chazit lelo Oref* [A Front without a Rearguard] (Tel Aviv: Yediot Ahronot, 2004).

30. Taken from the title of Netanel Lorch's *One Long War* (Jerusalem: Keter, 1976).

31. As late as 1993, direct contacts with any member or representative of the PLO was forbidden by Israeli law and subject to prosecution.

32. There is a growing body of autobiographical material dealing with Israeli-Arab diplomacy and negotiation, although unfortunately most of it relates to procedures and substance with very little discussion or even mention of cultural factors. In addition to those personal accounts referenced in this chapter, other insightful studies, in English, are as follows: on Egypt, Major-General Avraham Tamir, *A Soldier in Search of Peace: An Insider's Look at Israel's Strategy in the Middle East* (New York: Harper & Row, 1988); on Syria, Itamar Rabinovich, *The Brink of Peace* (Princeton, NJ: Princeton University Press, 1998); on Lebanon, David Kimche, *The Last Option* (New York: Macmillan, 1991); and on Jordan, Moshe Zak, "Israeli-Jordanian Negotiations," *Washington Quarterly* 8, no. 1 (Winter 1985): 167–176, which is the forerunner to his more extensive and detailed chronicle in Hebrew, *Hussein Oseh Shalom* [King Hussein Makes Peace: Thirty Years of Secret Talks], (Ramat Gan: Bar-Ilan University Press, 1994).

33. The description of Arafat comes from Abba Eban, *Diplomacy for the Next Century* (New Haven, CT: Yale University Press, 1998), 151.

34. Uri Savir, *The Process: 1,100 Days That Changed the Middle East* (New York: Random House, 1998), 315.

35. Ibid., 309.

36. Ibid., 102.

37. Ibid., 31.

38. Ehud Barak, "Speech to the National Defense College" (August 12, 1999) (http://wwww.israel.org/mfa/go).

39. Barak, quoted by *Haaretz* reporter Yossi Verter, March 6, 1998.

40. Omar Dajani, quoted in Annette Young, "Palestinian Idealist Says It's Time to Get Out," *Haaretz,* April 7, 2003, B3.

41. On the uses and abuses of intentional diplomatic vagueness, see the author's *Constructive Ambiguity in Middle East Peace-Making* (Tel Aviv: Tami Steinmetz Center for Peace Research, 1999). Also, see Anthony Wanis-St. John, "Back Channel Diplomacy: The Strategic Use of Multiple Channels of Negotiation in Middle East Peacemaking" (PhD diss., Fletcher School of Law and Diplomacy, April 2001).

42. Yossi Beilin, *Touching Peace: From the Oslo Accord to a Final Agreement* (London: Weidenfeld & Nicolson, 1999), 98.

43. The Israeli-Palestinian conspiracy of vagueness confirms the generalization made by Rubin and Brown that "it thus generally appears that bargainers who are high in tolerance for ambiguity are more likely to behave cooperatively than those who are low," except that the reverse is more likely, with those committed to cooperation most apt to fall back on ambiguity. Jeffrey Z. Rubin and Bert R. Brown, *The Social Psychology of Bargaining and Negotiation* (New York: Academic Press, 1975), 173 (chap. 7).

44. "Clinton Statement on Mideast Talks," *New York Times*, July 25, 2000 (http://www.nytimes.com).

45. Quoted in the *Jerusalem Post,* June 26, 2003. The phrase "that miserable summit" apears in Amnon Kapeliouk, "A Summit Clouded by Suspicion," *Ha'aretz*, November 23, 2001, B8.

46. In his study *Chinese Negotiating Behavior: Pursuing Interests through "Old Friends"* (Washington, DC: United States Institute of Peace Press, 1999), Richard H. Solomon alerts us to the likelihood of asymmetries in cross-political cultures. This focus is adopted, for example, by Israeli journalist Yossi Klein Halevy, who writes, "The deepest and most intractable asymmetry has been psychological: it has been an asymmetry of pity, or, more precisely, of self-pity. The Palestinians, as losers of the conflict, continue to see themselves solely as victims." "The Asymmetry of Pity," *National Interest* (Fall 2001): 38.

47. Shlomo Avineri, "Irreconcilable Differences," *Foreign Policy* (March-April 2002): 78. For Avineri, only part of the irreconcilable differences arise from Arab and Jewish cultures; the main problem is the tangible issues at stake: land, water, roads, Jerusalem neighborhoods, and so forth.

48. "End of a Journey," interview with Shlomo Ben-Ami by Ari Shavit, *Haaretz,* September 14, 2001, also excerpted in Saul Singer, "Camp David, Real and Invented," *Middle East Quarterly* (Spring 2002): 3–12.

49. "Clinton Statement on Mideast Talks," 9.

50. Ibid., 1.

51. Janice Gross Stein, "Image, Identity, and the Resolution of Violent Conflict," in *Turbulent Peace: The Challenges of Managing International Conflict,* ed. Chester A. Crocker, Fen Osler Hampson, and Pamela Aall (Washington, DC: United States Institute of Peace Press, 2001), 190.

52. The single best description of Arafat's Camp David ordeal remains Akram Hanieh, "The Camp David Papers," *Journal of Palestine Studies* 30, no. 118 (Winter 2001): 75–97.

53. See Benny Morris, "An Interview with Ehud Barak," part of a series of pieces on "Camp David and After: An Exchange" published by *New York Review of Books.* Barak rested his case by quoting Bill Clinton's remark to him: "Arafat refused even to accept it [the American proposal] as a basis for negotiations, walked out of the room, and deliberately turned to terrorism. That's the real story —all the rest is gossip." The Barak interview is in vol. 49, no. 10 (June 13, 2002). The onus for failure is also put on Arafat by Gilead Sher, one of Barak's closest confidants and principal negotiators, in his account in Hebrew of the proceedings. Gilead Sher, *B'merchak Negi'a* [Just beyond Reach] (Tel Aviv: Yediot Aharonot, 2001).

54. Ross has aired his strong criticism of Arafat on any number of public occasions. In March 2001, he described him as "long on complaints but short on prescriptions." Clyde Haberman, "Dennis Ross's Exit Interview," *New York Times*, March 25, 2001. Later that year he added, "I simply do not believe he is capable of doing a permanent status deal." "Camp David: An Exchange," *New York Review of Books*, September 20, 2001. Then, interviewed on the Fox News Channel on April 21, 2002, Ross accused Arafat of rejectionism, of never himself having raised a single idea during the fifteen days at Camp David, and concluded: "For him [Arafat] to end the conflict is to end himself."

55. Solomon, *Chinese Negotiating Behavior,* 162.

56. Robert Jervis, *Perception and Misperception in International Politics* (Princeton, NJ: Princeton University Press, 1976). Answering his own question, "Do the decision-maker's perceptions matter?" he stresses that "policies and decisions must be mediated by statesmen's goals, calculations, and perceptions" (13).

57. This can be seen, for instance, in the work of Michael Barnett, who insists "actors are embedded in and circumscribed by a normative structure" and employs a trinity of concepts—identity, narratives, and frames—within Israel's institutional context to show how cultural foundations, rather than human initiative, are what create a cultural space in national politics. Michael Barnett, "Culture, Strategy, and Foreign Policy Change: Israel's Road to Oslo," *European Journal of International Relations* 5, no. 1 (1999): 5–36.

58. Henry Kissinger, *Does America Need a Foreign Policy?* (New York: Simon & Schuster, 2001), 175.

59. "Clinton Statement on Mideast Talks," 2.

60. "Grasping for Peace," *Foreign Policy* (January-February 2002): 84.

61. Subsequently published as Ron Pundak, "From Oslo to Taba: What Went Wrong?" *Survival* 43, no. 3 (Autumn 2001): 31–46.

62. Reuven Merhav, "The Camp David Summit, 2000: What Went Wrong? —Lessons for the Future" (remarks delivered at a Tel Aviv University symposium, June 16–18, 2003, transcript courtesy of Professor Shimon Shamir and The University Institute for Diplomacy and Regional Cooperation).

63. Sher, *B'merchak Negi'a;* and Ben-Ami, *Chazit lelo Oref.*

64. Raymond Cohen, *Negotiating across Cultures: International Communication in an Interdependent World* (Washington, DC: United States Institute of Peace Press, 1997), 225. Elaborating on Cohen's distinction, Ginat generalizes, "On a purely behavioral level, Israelis are considered to be far more informal, frank, and direct—behavior that borders on arrogance and tactlessness. The Palestinians are more ceremonial, formal, polite, and less open." Joseph Ginat, introduction to *The Middle East Peace Process,* ed. Joseph Ginat, Edward J. Perkins, and Edwin G. Coor (Brighton, UK, and Portland, OR: Sussex Academic Press, 2002), 10.

Aware of Arafat's need for recognition and deep satisfaction from any public respect conferred upon him, Peres, Beilin, and even Rabin were far more amenable to symbolic gestures toward the *rais.* Nor had Barak's own two "negotiation encounters" with Arafat prior to Camp David, at the Erez checkpoint on July 11 and 27, 1999, gone particularly smoothly. Suggesting that something was badly out of synch, by the time Barak got around to making a personal gesture of goodwill by his celebrated hosting of Arafat at his home in Kochav Yair on September 25, 2000—two months *after* the summit—it was too late for the personal touch to salvage Barak's diplomacy.

65. Cohen, *Negotiating across Cultures,* 109.

66. I. William Zartman, *The 50% Solution* (Garden City, NY: Anchor Press, 1976).

67. In his detailed and colorful depiction of what transpired behind the scenes at Camp David, Akram Hanieh describes attempts by the American hosts at building social relations between the negotiators, including casual dress, taking meals together, allowing the delegations to mingle and chat informally, and leaving room for chance encounters in the exercise room and on the walking trails. On one occasion the two sides were invited to a basketball game, but as none of the Palestinians showed up, the Israelis ended up playing with the Marines who guarded the compound. Hanieh, "The Camp David Papers," 77.

68. Eban, *Diplomacy for the Next Century,* 142.

69. See Special Report no. 94, *U.S. Negotiating Behavior,* issued by the United States Institute of Peace (Washington, DC, October 2002).

70. See, for instance, Jeswald W. Salacuse, "Ten Ways That Culture Affects Negotiating Style: Some Survey Results," *Negotiation Journal* (July 1998): 221–239.

71. Ralph K. White, "Misperception in Vienna on the Eve of World War I," in *International War: An Anthology,* 2d ed., ed. Melvin Small and J. David Singer (Chicago: Dorsey Press, 1989), 256.

72. Charles Enderlin, *Shattered Dreams: The Failure of the Peace Process in the Middle East, 1995–2002* (New York: Other Press, 2003), 178, 214, 241.

73. Hussein Agha and Robert Malley, "Camp David: The Tragedy of Errors," *New York Review of Books*, August 9, 2001, 2–4, 5. Also, Hanieh, "The Camp David Papers," 93.

74. Agha and Malley, "Camp David," 10. Lee Ross adds a gloss by noting how "reactive devaluation" comes about because the "very act of offering a compromise or a concession seems to decrease its attractiveness in the eyes of the recipient." Lee Ross, "Psychological Barriers in Conflict Resolution," in *The Arab-Israeli Negotiations,* ed. Robin Twite and Tamar Herman (Tel Aviv: Papyrus, 1993), 172.

75. *Haaretz,* January 29, 2001.

76. Note that Israel's Taba delegation was headed by Foreign Minister Ben-Ami, Justice Minister Beilin, and former minister of education Yossi Sarid, who went beyond Camp David II, pushing back Israel's "red lines" still further by offering additional concessions on each of the three cardinal issues: territorial withdrawal, Jerusalem, and "the right of return." All three officials, interestingly, were prominent members of the peace camp and outside the loop of the dominant security subculture.

77. Shimon Peres and Arye Naor, *The New Middle East* (New York: Henry Holt, 1993).

78. Mahmoud Abbas, *Through Secret Channels* (Reading, UK: Garnet Publishing, 1995), 111.

79. Hanieh, "The Camp David Papers," 97.

80. Quoted by Benny Morris, from his "An Interview with Barak," 2.

81. Ibid., 9.

82. Ibid., 199 (emphasis mine).

5

Conclusion

❖❖❖❖❖❖❖❖❖❖❖❖❖❖❖❖

Culture as an

❖❖❖❖❖❖❖❖❖❖❖❖❖

Intervening Variable

❖❖❖❖❖❖❖❖❖❖❖❖❖❖❖❖❖❖❖❖❖

Tamara Cofman Wittes

T he foregoing analysis suggests that the influence of cultural factors on the Oslo negotiations was pervasive, operating at the individual, societal, and strategic levels. Moreover, the mechanisms by which culture and, specifically, national narratives shaped these different levels of politics suggest that culture might fruitfully be integrated into the scholarly understanding, not only of the Israeli-Palestinian negotiations, but of other interethnic negotiations as well, in Northern Ireland, Cyprus, Sri Lanka, the Caucasus, and elsewhere.

Omar Dajani's chapter on the Palestine Liberation Organization (PLO) sees culture's main effects at the level of domestic politics. He argues that the Palestinian cultural narrative—specifically, the communal Palestinian experiences of *nakba,* occupation, and self-government—deeply shaped the institutional structure of Palestinian politics, producing a fractious, competitive, and indecisive leadership that lacked domestic legitimacy. Internal competition made Palestinian negotiators extremely vulnerable to outbidding by more hard-line actors in domestic debates. It also made them loath to share information with one another or to coordinate positions prior to talks with Israeli representatives. This institutional structure gave extraordinary weight to Yasser Arafat, who retained sole authority to judge among competing factions, disburse resources, and approve negotiating policies and plans. Arafat's preference to keep all actors in play by never fully resolving disputes between his subordinates exacerbated the competitive dynamics described above. In sum, the disunity caused by Palestinians' historical discontinuity left their negotiators ill equipped to undertake detailed negotiations or to offer meaningful compromises on implementation and final-status issues, and disinclined to try.

Palestinian internal disunity and Arafat's central authority facilitated secret back-channel talks such as those that produced the original Oslo agreements. But once the interim period began, publicity was inevitable and domestic political competition became a major influence on Palestinian negotiating behavior in the final-status talks with Israel. The historical narrative of Palestinian nationalism, and its interweaving with both Muslim identity and the broader political movement of pan-Arabism, Dajani writes, made the discussion of particular issues with Israel (such as the return of refugees and the holy sites in Jerusalem) extraordinarily complex and fraught with political risk both domestic and regional. In other words, Palestinians' identity, forged as it was through the conflict with Zionism and the creation of the state of Israel, thoroughly conditioned the domestic politics, preferences, leadership, and negotiating style of the Palestinian side throughout the Oslo process.

Aharon Klieman's analysis also examines the influence of culture on domestic institutions, but Klieman demonstrates how that cultural influence affected the personalities of individual political leaders as they grappled with the implications of coexistence and a two-state solution to the conflict. Klieman views Israel's negotiating behavior in the Oslo process as presenting the "external manifestations of an ongoing internal struggle for policy dominance" between a national security subculture and a much weaker diplomatic subculture.

Klieman argues that, while the political landscape of many countries features a national security subculture, in the case of Israel that subculture is overwhelming in its size, power, and presence within governmental institutions and in the deference paid to it by political leaders, the public, and the media. Klieman attributes this dominance to Israel's cultural narrative of intense vulnerability and self-help, which was developed in the context of the experience not only of the Arab-Israeli war but also of European anti-Semitism. The resonance of this national security outlook within the Israeli body politic has enabled Israeli military and intelligence institutions to acquire impressive budgetary, bureaucratic, and political stature. It also means that political leaders who have best exemplified the national security subculture (especially former high-ranking military officers) have consistently won decisive electoral majorities. With its political resonance and bureaucratic heft, the national security subculture has heavily conditioned political leaders' decision making regarding negotiations with the PLO.

Klieman details how a small group of (about twenty) negotiators, comprising midlevel officials and associated unofficial advisers, attempted throughout the talks to limit the influence of the national security subculture by fostering an alternative style characterized by "the Oslo spirit." However, as Klieman points out, this diplomatic counternarrative—which saw Israel's security as reliant on normalized relations with its neighbors and the world community—never fully influenced the top Israeli leadership, as the national security subculture still dominated both personalities and domestic political calculations. As negotiations progressed and higher levels of the Israeli political establishment became more engaged in the talks, a degree of "cultural unlearning" took place, whereby the summiteers' security-driven perceptions of the issues overwhelmed the talks and contributed to the extraordinary clash of wills and worldviews between Yasser Arafat and Ehud Barak at the Camp David summit in July 2000.

Israeli and Palestinian Interaction: Reinforcing Each Other's Worst Traits

Reading Klieman's and Dajani's accounts together, one can clearly see how the national security approach that dominated Israel's negotiating style and the passivity and indecision that characterized the Palestinian side interacted in a tremendously counterproductive fashion and contributed to the conflagration during and after the summit at Camp David. The vicious cycle began after the first Oslo agreement, when publicity led domestic politics to become a larger part of each side's decision-making equation, and when Israeli negotiators who embraced the "spirit of Oslo" were supplemented and in some cases replaced by professional military and intelligence officials, so that the national security subculture began to dominate the Israeli team. Given their passivity, along with their relative lack of preparation and less-than-professional internecine warfare, the Palestinians were particularly vulnerable to the security hawks' favored tactics of divide and rule and pressing the advantage.

The Israelis' willingness to take advantage of the Palestinian team's weaknesses led the Palestinians to feel burdened by the interim agreements that resulted from the first two years' talks and pressured to reach a more equitable deal in the final-status agreement. Israel's security subculture led its negotiators to lay numerous and absolute "red lines" in the interim talks and to defend them aggressively and without compromise. As Dajani relates, the Palestinians felt railroaded as a result, leading them to adopt a strategy in final-status talks of negotiating from principles rather than specific substantive positions. Israel's negotiators viewed this Palestinian emphasis on principles as a maddening refusal to grapple with key issues and as a preference for dwelling in the past over embracing a future of negotiated coexistence.

Internal divisions left the Palestinians without clear red lines or fallback positions on entering the final-status talks, forcing them to use Israeli proposals as catalysts for their own internal debates on issues that had previously been taboo. Israelis, meanwhile, viewed this inability to respond as evidence of a lack of serious intent in the negotiations. This played into already-extant Israeli suspicions of their interlocutors' insincerity, cultivated by their history in the region and by their broader historical narrative of being a besieged minority in a hostile environment.

Outside the immediate confines of the negotiating room, the analysis of Israeli and Palestinian negotiating styles in this volume also demonstrates how both sides' cultural baggage influenced their interpretations of and responses to the relative balance of power between them, and the negotiating strategies they developed in response to this perceived balance. Reading Dajani's and Klieman's analyses together reveals how, as Klieman points out, "a good deal of the tragedy arises from . . . being so much and too much alike." In other words, the national narratives of the two sides parallel each other in ways that made them interact particularly badly in discussion of issues that did, after all, concern the existential viability of their communities. Each side's national identity is rooted in a sense of minority status, persecution, vulnerability, and unrelieved threat. Each side felt itself to be the disadvantaged and weaker one—Israel with respect to the surrounding Arab region, the Palestinians with respect to Israel's military, economic, and territorial dominance within historic Palestine. It is interesting to note that this "double-minority" aspect of the Israeli-Palestinian conflict also appears in other ethnic conflicts, such as those in Cyprus and Northern Ireland.[1]

These parallel views led both sides to believe that the other should bear the burden for concessions in the talks. Palestinians felt that Israel's physical dominance of mandatory Palestine and the PLO's prior acceptance of a two-state solution put the burden for concessions on the Israeli side. During the interim talks, Israeli negotiators, in a view reinforced by the national security subculture, felt that the PLO should yield more concessions because it had so few cards to play and had proven to be disorganized and unprofessional in its internal management of Palestinian affairs. In the final-status talks, however, Israel's culturally ingrained sense of weakness weighed heavily. Israeli negotiators, even those infused with the diplomatic subculture, saw a Palestinian settlement as the key to "normalizing" Israel's status in the region, transforming it from a pariah David against the Arab Goliath into a legitimate partner in building a "new Middle East." When Yasser Arafat at Camp David cited pan-Arab and pan-Islamic concerns as preventing him from compromising on Jerusalem, denied any Jewish claim to the Temple Mount, and insisted on the Palestinian right of return, the Israelis questioned their state's existential viability under a two-state solution and wondered whether normalization of Israel's status as a Jewish state in its homeland was a pipe dream that the Palestinians simply could not (or would not) deliver. At the same time, the Israelis' steamroller approach at Camp David and refusal to grapple with issues of principle regarding refugees and borders led the Palestinian side to believe that one of their key symbolic goals in the talks—the recognition by Israel (and the world) of the legitimacy of the Palestinian narrative of victimization—was likewise unachievable.

These parallels in Israeli and Palestinian national identity, and correspondingly in their perceptions of their strategic environment, meant that the negotiators had particularly high obstacles to overcome in intercultural communication, and they failed more often than they succeeded. Moreover, each team's weaknesses and flaws, many of which were culturally shaped, reinforced the prejudices and fears of the other side, producing a downward spiral in the effectiveness of each side's negotiating style from the signing of the Oslo agreement to the collapse of the final-status talks. In this way, tragically, the culturally shaped styles of Israeli and Palestinian negotiators and culturally shaped perceptions of the balance of power and the threat environment combined at Camp David with mismatched personalities and the substantive thorniness of the issues at stake to produce a dramatic failure that undermined the fundamental confidence of both sides that a peace agreement was indeed in their nations' best interests.

Culture as an Intervening Variable

As noted in the introductory chapter, this volume does not intend to use culture as an alternative explanation for the failure of the Oslo peace process, competing for relevance with leaders' personalities, domestic politics, or the balance of power between Israel and the Palestinians. Instead, this volume argues for the relevance of culture to all three of these primary levels of analysis: individual, domestic, and international. This volume maintains that cultural factors influenced, among other things,

- the identity, strategy, and preferences of the political leadership in Israel and the PLO;

- the cohesion, style, and mandate of Israeli and Palestinian negotiating teams;

- the domestic institutions that shaped national policy on the conflict under negotiation and the conduct of the talks themselves;

- the domestic political environment within which each political leadership had to maneuver while negotiating with the other;

- the ability and incentives (of the Palestinian side in particular) to refer to or make use of third parties as a tactic in the talks; and

- each side's perception of their strategic environment, especially the balance of power between them, and their responses to that perceived balance.

In other words, the authors of this volume reveal the impact of cultural factors on every level of analysis—individual, domestic, and international —relevant to the negotiation of this intercommunal dispute. The breadth of culture's influence across levels of analysis suggests that *culture is most appropriately viewed not as an independent variable* in explaining negotiating outcomes but as an important intervening variable that shapes the impact of major independent variables on the talks.

To explore more completely what this notion of culture as an intervening variable means in practice, we will now return to several commonly advanced explanations for the failure of the Oslo process that have emerged in the extant literature on the talks and have been discussed over the course of the preceding chapters. By revealing culture's role in each of these competing explanations, we will demonstrate what the addition of a cultural lens contributes to our understanding of the Israeli-Palestinian talks and our understanding of what will be necessary for them to successfully negotiate an end to their conflict.

Explanation I: It's Just Too Hard

The first explanation for the ultimate failure of the Oslo process concerns the substance of the negotiations: the issues at stake in the final-status negotiations were just too complex and difficult to enable agreement to be reached (see chapter 2). Undoubtedly, even two teams with no direct stake in the outcome would have found it difficult to draft arrangements for power sharing in Jerusalem's patchwork of Arab and Jewish neighborhoods; for the return, compensation, or resettlement of millions of Palestinian refugees; or for untangling competing needs at contested holy sites such as the Haram al-Sharif/Temple Mount. Our analysis argues that the complexity of negotiating these issues was compounded many times over by the effects of culture:

- Cultural assumptions regarding holy sites and religious history and their resonance in Palestinian domestic politics led Arafat to deny a Jewish claim to the Temple Mount during the Camp David talks, shocking the Israeli team and deepening their suspicion that he was not negotiating toward coexistence in good faith.

- The culturally influenced dysfunctions of the Palestinian negotiating team and the intense resonance of the refugee issue within the Palestinian body politic combined to make the issue a "hot potato" for which no Palestinian politician had incentive to put forward a potential solution.

- In a parallel fashion, the extreme threat perception among Israelis (that Palestinians wished to use the refugee return to impugn the moral legitimacy of Israel's creation and to demographically reverse the Jewishness of the Jewish state) made compromise on the issue tremendously difficult for Israel.

Explanation II: Personality over All

Others, including Klieman, note the importance of personalities in the negotiations—the truculence of Yasser Arafat in failing to negotiate for an end to the conflict[2] and the different Israeli negotiating approaches evident under Prime Ministers Yitzhak Rabin, Shimon Peres, Binyamin Netanyahu, and Ehud Barak. Here, too, culture is relevant, as Klieman's chapter shows:

- The security subculture of Israel and Israeli politics deeply shaped the political viability of potential leaders in Israeli politics (advantaging those with strong military credentials), as well as influencing the approaches of individual Israeli prime ministers to the negotiations.

- The resonance of security arguments in Israeli society and the vulnerability to opposition parties of any Israeli government that compromised in the name of peace was something to which each of the Israeli prime ministers during the Oslo process was acutely sensitive, though they dealt with the problem in different ways and with varying degrees of success.

- The resonance of security arguments with the Israeli public meant that prime ministers with weaker security credentials (e.g., Peres and Netanyahu) were more vulnerable to accusations of endangering security, and therefore more constrained in the negotiations by domestic political calculations, than their counterparts who had served as senior military officers (e.g., Rabin and Barak).

Explanation III: It's All about Communication

Finally, there is the argument that would be applied to the Israeli-Palestinian process by the existing literature on intercultural negotiations: the problem with the final stages of the Oslo talks was a problem of communication, and the common language and common set of assumptions that had been built among the narrow group of negotiators who met in Oslo during 1993 was lost as the negotiating teams expanded and the Israeli governments changed. This argument suggests that successful negotiations demand the triumph of a common negotiating culture over the problem of intercultural communications.

There is good evidence that the small teams who met repeatedly over months in Oslo built a common language and a common view of their task that enabled them to overcome obstacles. However, it is equally true that the Oslo talks, in their secrecy and their substance—negotiating a set of broad overarching principles to guide later negotiations in a gradualist process—artificially distanced the negotiating teams from the realities that governed both the conflict and the prospects for its negotiated resolution. For example, the Oslo teams agreed in one of their first meetings to set aside all discussion of history, a move possible only when final-status issues such as borders were also set aside. Moreover, because of the negotiators' isolation from domestic political pressures (where cultural factors operated to constrain the negotiations in later stages), and because of the interim nature of the agreement being negotiated, the Oslo talks moved swiftly past precisely those issues and obstacles that were most fraught with each side's social-psychological baggage: settlements, refugees, Jerusalem, and so on. As Klieman's previous work has noted, the "constructive ambiguity" embraced by the negotiators in Oslo enabled an agreement, but that agreement failed to achieve any common understanding on key issues. Those covered-over differences, in interpretation and in assumptions about how the negotiating process would proceed, ended up having a significant impact, as Dajani's chapter details, on each side's approach to the final-status talks, creating unrealistically high expectations on both sides.

In other words, to the extent that the early negotiations in Oslo succeeded in overcoming culturally shaped barriers to effective negotiation and mutual agreement, they did so by setting aside substantive issues that would have to be resolved in some fashion before a final agreement could be signed. The Oslo-era talks, then, did not triumph over cultural differences; rather, the talks ignored those differences and narrowed the scope of the negotiations to enable this artificial environment to be sustained. The closer the two sides came to final-status talks, the more difficult it became to insulate the negotiations from these culturally shaped realities.

What Does a Cultural Perspective Add to Negotiations Theory?

Illuminating the cultural influence on individual decision makers, institutional structure, and threat perception helps us to see how the interaction between these levels of analysis affected the outcome of the Israeli-Palestinian talks. In particular, the preceding chapters focus on the influence of Israeli and Palestinian "national narratives"—the tales each community tells itself and teaches its children about its history, current environment, and future (and threats to that future). The parallels are painfully clear. The history of both Jews and Palestinians left each group with a fundamental obsession with obtaining external validation and recognition of their national identities and national claims. Because both groups claimed authentic ties to the same land, each saw the other's national claims as an existential threat to its own. Peaceful dispute resolution for Israelis and Palestinians demands more than the creation of a mutually acceptable border: it requires mutual recognition and long-term coexistence. Because of this, each side's threat perception was and remains extraordinarily high and felt throughout the body politic.

Culture, and the interethnic nature of the conflict, thus seems to have affected the very goal of negotiations. It is worth emphasizing Dajani's point that, for Palestinians and the PLO, the negotiations were not meant only to end the conflict and provide for Palestinian statehood but also to provide for a kind of recognition and vindication of the Palestinian national narrative. For this essentially symbolic Palestinian goal to be achieved, the Israeli team would have had to go much further—acknowledging some responsibility for the creation of the refugee problem, for example —than most Israelis were willing to go. The more salient this goal of vindication became for Palestinians, the more Israelis saw Palestinian demands as an attempt to use the talks to negate the legitimacy of Israel's existence in the region. In this sense, culture—in the form of attitudes toward the recognition and legitimization of each side's national identity—played a large role in scuttling the final-status talks and, moreover, in hardening the attitudes of both Israeli and Palestinian publics following the failure of the Camp David summit.[3]

As our analysis of the Israeli-Palestinian talks demonstrates, in negotiations between rival communal groups over the terms of coexistence, the domestic political context is strongly colored by the domestic narrative of the conflict and the identities of self and other at stake in it. This cultural influence is felt in party and electoral politics, and in the behavior of interest groups and other actors. Moderating one's negotiating positions to make an agreement possible always carries domestic political costs for leaders, and in every security-related negotiation, leaders are vulnerable to the accusation of having betrayed the national interest. But in negotiations between ethnic rivals, the very act of negotiation itself is often viewed as an act of disloyalty or betrayal because negotiation implies acceptance of the other's existence, and this acknowledgment is seen in the zero-sum context of ethnic conflict as devaluing or endangering the existence and national rights of one's own community. It is not simply a question of relative gains—in ethnic conflicts, any gain by the adversary is viewed as tantamount to existential disaster. This volume's findings suggest that, because of this additional cultural burden, negotiations in ethnic conflicts are much more sensitive to domestic politics than are other types of negotiations. Moreover, the domestic debate over negotiations and coexistence is thoroughly steeped in the language of culture and the manipulation by various sides of key cultural symbols.[4] Both Dajani and Klieman note the influence of cultural narratives on the broader Israeli and Palestinian public perceptions of the negotiations and of the adversary's intentions, and thereby on the domestic political environment in which the talks took place. Both authors detail how public perceptions of the ongoing negotiations influenced the preferences and calculations of Israeli and Palestinian political leaders as the talks progressed, especially in constraining each side's "red lines" in the final-status talks in 2000.

The extreme sensitivity of interethnic negotiations such as the Oslo process to domestic politics, and especially to outbidding of pro-peace political leaders by domestic extremists, suggests the critical importance of public diplomacy to a successful Israeli-Palestinian peace process. The importance of public diplomacy and its failures in the Oslo process are perhaps best illustrated by the fact that the most successful negotiations in the Israeli-Palestinian peace process occurred via a secret back channel, where two small delegations met over time without public disclosure. In contrast, the most public summitry of the Oslo process produced its biggest failures.

Lessons for Negotiators

How can political leaders and negotiators make use of this volume's insights into culture and intercommunal negotiations? Five recommendations flow from the preceding analysis.

First, history is important. In Israeli-Palestinian negotiations, each team's view and use of history in the negotiations led the other side to doubt their commitment to coexistence. On the Israeli side, as Omar Dajani discusses, the rejection of Palestinian attempts to discuss history led Palestinians to conclude that Israel had not come to terms with its role in the conflict and in Palestinians' plight. On the Palestinian side, Arafat's cavalier treatment of Jewish history in the holy land during the Camp David discussions shocked both the Israelis and the American mediators and added to their concerns about his ability to accept and implement a negotiated compromise. Thus, a clear conclusion of this study is the need for negotiators, including those at the most senior levels, to not simply familiarize themselves with the other party's historical narrative, but to understand how that narrative shapes the other party's negotiating preferences today. History cannot be ignored in negotiation of a communal conflict: achieving at least some understanding of and agreement on the two communities' shared history is probably necessary to avoid a situation in which assumptions about history expressed in negotiating positions are misinterpreted as evidence of bad faith or intentions. If interethnic negotiations are in part about recognition and validation of each side's identity claims, recognition of a shared history is a relatively "cheap" means of achieving that symbolic goal.

Considering the Palestinian refugee problem in this light, for example, yields a difficult but perhaps important insight for negotiators to confront. The refugees are embodiments of the Palestinian narrative of dispossession, and making the refugees "whole" again through some honorable recognition of and compensation for the wrong done to them is a necessary part of normalizing Palestinian national identity. Of course, coming to terms with the way in which some Palestinians became refugees in 1948 would involve a degree of revision in the Israeli national narrative that some Israelis would find threatening, as it erodes the moral purity of the state's establishment. However, if the Jewish claim to a national homeland is strong enough on its own terms, as most native-born Israeli Jews instinctively and reflexively believe, then it can accommodate the fact (as, indeed, has American national identity) that the national homeland was not created without paying a moral price.

Second, the effects of culture on domestic politics present a tremendous barrier to successful negotiations that the two negotiating teams and their political leaders must work together to overcome. In this case, the impact of culture was most clearly seen in the dysfunction of the Palestinian decision-making process. The Israeli willingness to take advantage of internal Palestinian divisions led to unbalanced agreements and ultimately assisted in the demise of the PLO as a legitimate or credible negotiator in the eyes of its own population and most Israelis. Israeli leaders and negotiators clearly failed to respond in the most appropriate, self-interested way to Palestinian political dynamics. As this volume has amply demonstrated, pressing that advantage may produce a better immediate outcome for Israel but in the long term produces failure. *To achieve a successful agreement that can survive implementation, Israeli negotiators must help Palestinians overcome their leadership gaps, rather than exploiting them in the name of expediency and getting a better deal.* This requires Israel to actively yield some of its natural advantages in negotiating with the Palestinians, an action that goes directly against the grain of Israel's security-dominated negotiating style. To counsel this approach is not necessarily to accept the Palestinian claim that the burden must be on Israel to offer the majority of concessions in order for negotiations to succeed.

Greater awareness on the Israeli side of how the Palestinian national movement's history and its interaction with Zionism and Israel have shaped the movement's leadership and institutions would enable Israel to better gauge its negotiating style and to assist the most productive and relevant Palestinian factions in using the negotiations to gain the upper hand in internal politics. This would not only promote more successful negotiations and more stable agreements but also help ensure Israel's long-term interest in the emergence of a legitimate, moderate Palestinian leadership. This approach can be contrasted with the current Israeli policy of insisting on unitary and responsible Palestinian decision making by leaders who are themselves dependent on and handicapped by the existing institutional structure of power and thus incapable of making, much less implementing, such decisions.

For their part, *Palestinian negotiators must recognize the systemic, deeply embedded nature of what they acknowledge is a dysfunctional negotiating style* and take appropriate steps to correct it. The repeated failure of the PLO team to present a coherent and proactive negotiating position cannot be explained simply by inadequate preparation, temporary political constraints, or even individual preferences. Rather, as Dajani shows, this failing must be understood as part of the institutional dysfunction of the PLO as a whole. Thus, Palestinian leaders and activists interested in successful negotiations with Israel must work for a fundamental political accord among the Palestinian leadership concerning negotiations with Israel. Without clear and agreed-upon positions and the ability to present ideas and avoid the passivity that plagued past discussions, Palestinian negotiators cannot successfully press for the accommodation of Palestinian interests in final-status talks with Israel.

The above two recommendations may be too ambitious. At the very least, however, the findings of this volume suggest that *the next round of serious Palestinian-Israeli engagement must be preceded by a long and quiet pre-negotiation phase,* during which time the Palestinians will have to resolve internal divisions over basic questions regarding the relationship with Israel and the Israelis will have to make a significant and sustained effort to understand the long-term interests and concerns of their interlocutors. Although one can identify a process of pre-negotiation that led up to the 1993 Declaration of Principles, that process was focused on prerequisites for mutual recognition. The next phase of pre-negotiation must be *focused on the prerequisites for long-term coexistence.*

A third recommendation that springs from the preceding chapters is that *the task of overcoming the obstacles domestic politics creates for agreement in interethnic disputes requires a broader form of cooperative confidence building.* Formal negotiations will benefit from constant informal coordination between the two sides on the cultural and domestic political resonance of their actions. This cooperation will minimize the degree to which the talks are overwhelmed by negative dynamics operating between the two communities. While negotiations between communal competitors are often preceded or accompanied by a cease-fire, the cultural lens suggests that bloodshed is by no means the only negative development that can torpedo talks—insensitive treatment of a culturally resonant place (e.g., a holy site) or a speech by a leader that casts doubt on his good faith can do as much damage. The Israeli-Palestinian negotiations are replete with negative examples in this regard.

Fourth, *mediators and other third parties also have an important role to play in helping to overcome the barriers to agreement that culture can create.* Clinton's blindness to the roots of Palestinian passivity made him impatient with Arafat at Camp David and led him to misjudge Arafat's silence as a lack of sincerity—the same erroneous perception now regrettably embedded in the minds of most Israelis. A more sensitive American interlocutor would have been able to translate Arafat's behavior for Barak, and likewise Barak's behavior for Arafat, to whom Barak appeared arrogant, inflexible, and simultaneously increasingly desperate for a deal. Successful Israeli-Palestinian negotiations will require the active involvement of a third party who is not only committed to bridging substantive gaps between the parties but also sensitive to and able to remind each side of the other's culturally induced attitudes, positions, and negotiating styles.

The fifth and final recommendation concerns culture and the two-level game: Oftentimes, negotiators will use domestic political constraints as an excuse or a pressure tactic to wrench concessions from the other side. *Greater sensitivity by negotiators to the cultural resonance of particular issues under discussion will help the wise negotiator recognize when a claim of domestic constraints is a pressure tactic and when it is a genuine constraint that must be addressed jointly by the parties if the talks are to proceed.*

❖ ❖ ❖

Negotiations to end a violent conflict, especially one involving the competing claims of distinct national communities, will always be heated and adversarial. However, if the leadership on each side is persuaded of his counterpart's serious intent to negotiate peace, then at some point the negotiation must become a partnership as well as a confrontation. To succeed in building a common future of peaceful coexistence, Israeli and Palestinian leaders will have to work together to help each other overcome the inevitable barriers to agreement that their shared history of communal conflict has created. In focusing attention on the cultural barriers to peacemaking between Israelis and Palestinians, this volume's authors hope to contribute to more successful negotiations in years to come.

Notes

1. See the discussion of the "double-minority" problem in Stephen Ryan, *Ethnic Conflict and International Relations* (Brookfield, VT: Dartmouth, 1990).

2. Dennis Ross, for example, told the *New York Times,* "I have come to the conclusion that he is not capable of negotiating an end to the conflict because what is required of him is something he is not able to do." Clyde Haberman, "Dennis Ross's Exit Interview," *New York Times Magazine,* March 25, 2001, 36ff.

3. Herbert C. Kelman, "Israelis and Palestinians: Psychological Prerequisites for Mutual Acceptance," in *Religion, Culture, and Psychology in Arab-Israeli Relations,* ed. Ian Lustick (New York: Garland Press, 1994).

4. The continuous influence of the domestic sphere on international negotiations has been explored in the growing body of literature on negotiations as a two-level game. See Peter B. Evans and others, *Double-Edged Diplomacy: International Bargaining and Domestic Politics,* no. 25 in the series *Studies in International Political Economy* (Berkeley: University of California Press, 1993).

Index

How Israelis and Palestinians Negotiate

This book is set in Times New Roman. The Creative Shop designed the book's cover; Mike Chase designed the interior. Helene Y. Redmond made up the pages. The text was copyedited by Jennifer Scupi and proofread by Karen Stough. The index was prepared by Sonsie Conroy. The book's editor was Nigel Quinney.